Christmas by Candlelight

David Thomson

Other books by David Thomson

A Journey with John: A Holy Week Bible Study
(Authentic, £3.50) ISBN 1-85078-561-9

Lent with Luke
(Authentic, £5.99) ISBN 1-85078-597-X

Christmas by Candlelight

Readings and Reflections
From Advent to Epiphany

David Thomson

Authentic

First published 2006 by Authentic Lifestyle

Authentic Lifestyle is an imprint of Authentic Media,
9 Holdom Avenue, Bletchley, Milton Keynes, MK1 1QR, UK
and
P.O. Box 1047, Waynesboro, GA 30830-2047, U.S.A.

12 11 10 09 08 07 06   7 6 5 4 3 2 1

British Library Cataloguing in Publication Data
A catalogue record for this book is available from the British Library

ISBN–13: 978-1-85078-699-3
ISBN–10: 1-85078-699-2

Designed and typeset by Christopher Lawther, Teamwork, Lancing, West Sussex
and printed and bound in Great Britain by Bell and Bain, Glasgow

Contents

1st Sunday in Advent:

2nd Sunday in Advent:

3rd Sunday in Advent:

4th Sunday in Advent:

Christmas Day

The Epiphany

Acknowledgements

This is the third small book for which I have had the support and encouragement of Jeremy Mudditt as publisher and Chris Lawther as designer. What a team! I only hope that the contents, for which I have to take full responsibility, live up to the container.

Making the space in an archidiaconal diary for writing is quite a challenge. Without the holy space of Holy Name House at Keswick, which the sisters have made so generously available to me, it would never have got done. So thanks to them too for their hospitality and their prayers. I am grateful as well to my colleagues in the diocese and at the cathedral who have helped me keep the space I have made, and to all those who on quiet days and the like have unwittingly been partners in helping the material of this book come to birth.

A big thank you too to members of my family, especially my wife Jean and my father Ron (the truly venerable Canon Thomson) who have not only lived with the agonies of authorship, but been active conspirators in my imagining and writing.

Special thanks for this volume go, finally, to James Armstrong, Head Verger at Carlisle Cathedral, who has been a very willing collaborator in putting together the illustrations. The images marked JA in the list below are his, but he helped identify and set up many of the others too. The remainder are either my own or not, as far as I know, in copyright. I have only included those whose subjects are of interest or source needs specifying. The locations are in Carlisle Cathedral unless I say otherwise.

Introduction

This is a book to help you take time over Christmas to let Christ's light shine, in a season that is usually so busy that its real meaning gets lost in a maze of distractions.

A simple symbol of taking time to pray and connect with God is lighting a candle, and this has become a major part of our Christmas preparations today, at church and at home. It's not often that a TV programme sets the tone for a major development in worship, but I gather that *Blue Peter*, in fact, is probably responsible for the amazing popularity of Advent Candle wreaths today. Just take two coat-hangers … *

Our usual pattern is to light a candle for each of the four weeks of Advent, with perhaps a final one for Christmas itself. The candles have been interpreted in various ways, but the scheme embedded in the current liturgies and used here leads us from the Patriarchs to the Prophets to John the Baptist and finally to Mary and the Birth.

So with this book as your companion you are invited to spend a week reflecting on the pointers of promise that God has given us in the old tales of the Patriarchs; a week waking up to the alarm calls of the Prophets; a week preparing the way with Baptist; and a week around the Crib with Mary and the others.

You will find all the familiar Carol Service readings here to reflect on, as well as all the early chapters of Matthew and Luke's Gospels, and the prologue of St John's.

After Christmas these readings will lead us to the Epiphany, and in a final week continue the story right up to the end of Christ's childhood, so that Christmas does not stay for us just a celebration of a baby's birth, but becomes a launch-pad into the life of adult faith.

Christmas and Epiphany of course fall on various days of the week. There is a special page for each of them, and when you reach the feast day you can simply swap the material provided for it with what you would otherwise have been using. For the Sundays in Advent I have given you the Candle prayer for the week and a starter for the week's theme – but I assume you will be listening to wiser voices than mine in a Sunday Service in church or over the airwaves so I have kept it short!

Light shining in the darkness, God with us in the everyday, the unfolding of God's great purpose from Creation through to Culmination – these are the themes of Advent, when we call to mind God's coming in the beginning, in Christ, in us, and at the end.

Grand narratives like this are supposed to be out of favour in our post-modern world; but in fact they do not so easily lie down and die. Purpose and meaning are universals of our consciousness and our culture, and where there is no common account of them all sorts of uncommon ones are constructed. What we can encounter in this Advent journey, as we take the time to let it encounter us, is a real truth, the deep down meaning of things; and it can set us free.

At the heart of this book, then, is a prompt for each of us to take time this Advent – a little time each day would be best, the same time and place if you can. You could place a candle there to light each time too.

I have printed out the day's Bible reading, but it would not be a bad idea to have your own working Bible to hand there as well, and perhaps a notebook to keep a record of what God adds to your waiting.

At the end of each week's studies are some notes to help a study group in 'taking time together' (you could call your group that) – or to use on your own if you prefer.

The meaning is in the waiting. The Access credit card famously offered to take the waiting out of wanting, but Advent reminds us that waiting is not just postponement, not even just preparation, but something that adds value in its own right. Taking time is also redeeming the time. We put the spaces back between the words – so that we can hear the Word.

Now – time to put the waiting back into the wanting.

Prompt me, God
But not yet. When I speak
Though it be you who speak
Through me, something is lost.
The meaning is in the waiting.

R.S. Thomas*

Almighty God,
give us grace to cast away the works of darkness
and to put on the armour of light,
now in the time of this mortal life,
in which your Son Jesus Christ came to us in great humility;
that on the last day,
when he shall come again in his glorious majesty to judge the living
and the dead,
we may rise to the life immortal;
through him who is alive and reigns with you,
in the unity of the Holy Spirit,
one God, now and for ever. Amen

Collect for Advent Sunday*

The *Taking Time Together* notes for group studies are based on the simple model of a meal. There is an idea for a starter, another for the main course or main part of the time, and a third giving ideas for prayer to finish off the banquet. If you follow the book right through, you will have a six session course.

In fact, you could have the *Time Together* round a good meal, at least for one of the sessions: after all, this is Christmas not Lent! And don't just think evenings: the material isn't so heavy that you couldn't use it over a long coffee break, or at a shared Sunday lunch.

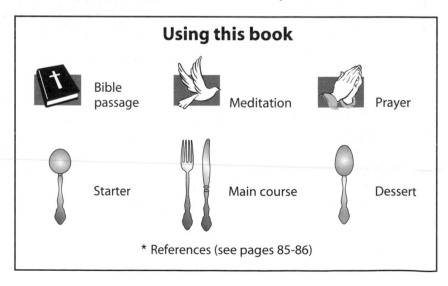

Using this book

Bible passage	Meditation	Prayer
Starter	Main course	Dessert

* References (see pages 85-86)

WEEK 1 — FIRST SUNDAY IN ADVENT

The Patriarchs – pointers of promise

Blessed are you, Sovereign Lord, God of our ancestors:
to you be praise and glory for ever!
You called the patriarchs to live by the light of faith
and to journey in the hope of your promised fulfilment.
May we be obedient to your call
and be ready and watchful to receive your Christ,
a lamp to our feet and a light to our path;
for you are our light and our salvation.
*Blessed be God for ever.**

The first candle in the Advent wreath is for the patriarchs – Noah, Abraham, Jacob, Moses – shadowy, heroic figures whose names come down to us from the dawn of our faith history. It is for the all-too-human lives they show us that are nevertheless wonderfully shot through with God's presence and

central to God's story. It is for the glimpses of the light that they have passed down to our also very human lives, as pointers of promise.

This is no short story that they and we are starting on, but the whole history of our creation and redemption. To find our place in that story we need to take time: time out, time to reflect, time to notice, time to be. So today take time and let all that is around and within you start to speak; and take it to the light and the light to it – because even though we think of the patriarchs as we light this first candle, its light is still the one light of Christ.

MONDAY

The Creation

Genesis 1.1, 2.4-9, 16-25

In the beginning God created the heavens and the earth.

This is the account of the heavens and the earth when they were created.

When the Lord God made the earth and the heavens – and no shrub of the field had yet appeared on the earth and no plant of the field had yet sprung up, for the Lord God had not sent rain on the earth and there was no man to work the ground, but streams came up from the earth and watered the whole surface of the ground – the Lord God formed the man from the dust of the ground and breathed into his nostrils the breath of life, and the man became a living being.

Now the Lord God had planted a garden in the east, in Eden; and there he put the man he had formed. And the Lord God made all kinds of trees grow out of the ground – trees that were pleasing to the eye and good for food. In the middle of the garden were the tree of life and the tree of the knowledge of good and evil.

And the Lord God commanded the man, "You are free to eat from any tree in the garden; but you must not eat from the tree of the knowledge of good and evil, for when you eat of it you will surely die."

The Lord God said, "It is not good for the man to be alone. I will make a helper suitable for him."

Now the Lord God had formed out of the ground all the beasts of the field and all the birds of the air. He brought them to the man to see what he would name them; and whatever the man called each living creature, that was its name. So the man gave names to all the livestock, the birds of the air and all the beasts of the field.

But for Adam no suitable helper was found. So the Lord God caused the man to fall into a deep sleep; and while he was sleeping, he took one of the man's ribs and closed up the place with flesh. Then the Lord God made a woman from the rib he had taken out of the man, and he brought her to the man.

The man said, "This is now bone of my bones and flesh of my flesh; she shall be called 'woman', for she was taken out of man."

For this reason a man will leave his father and mother and be united to his wife, and they will become one flesh.

The man and his wife were both naked, and they felt no shame.

Most of my childhood was spent in Sheffield, before the Clean Air Act came in, and I well remember feeling my way to school one day when the steelworks' smog was particularly bad. Bombsites were still all around us, and the only plant that did well was rosebay willow-herb.

Fast forward to a day twenty years' later in the Cotswolds when I was walking through the fields and suddenly it hit me – farming and gardening were not some alien activity but a way of joining in God's work of creation, taking its unruly plethora of potential and bringing order and fruitfulness out of it.

In the beginning – creation. The Creation and the Fall begin the traditional service of lessons and carols. But 'the beginning' are also the words with which two of the Gospels begin, so in the beginning – re-creation too. We see creation and re-creation in the sequence of time: but from the point of view of eternity they are one story, of the light shining in the darkness, and the darkness not overcoming it.

And in this creation and re-creation, women and men have a special part to play, co-creators with God in a continuing work that goes far beyond the first seven days. The special part we play is tied up with our nature that cannot just be good, but must choose good, knowingly. We are moral beings like God, and we become more like him and more really ourselves as we do consistently choose the good.

Like gardening and farming, this can be hard work, this cultivating of the soul. Souls too have both the potential to be stunningly beautiful, – and to produce an astonishing amount of prunings and weeds. Leave them, and they soon revert to jungle. Tend them, and they can be like heaven.

How does your garden grow?
How is a human to grow true?
How to be good?
How to be pruned?
Here, Lord, is my garden:
Come and walk with me in it again,
And teach my now-knowing heart
To be like you
And become truly me.

TUESDAY

The Fall

Genesis 3.8-15

Then the man and his wife heard the sound of the Lord God as he was walking in the garden in the cool of the day, and they hid from the Lord God among the trees of the garden. But the Lord God called to the man, "Where are you?"

He answered, "I heard you in the garden, and I was afraid because I was naked; so I hid."

And he said, "Who told you that you were naked? Have you eaten from the tree from which I commanded you not to eat?"

The man said, "The woman you put here with me – she gave me some fruit from the tree, and I ate it."

Then the Lord God said to the woman, "What is this you have done?"

The woman said, "The serpent deceived me, and I ate."

So the Lord God said to the serpent, "Because you have done this,

"Cursed are you above all the livestock and all the wild animals!
You will crawl on your belly
and you will eat dust
all the days of your life.
And I will put enmity
between you and the woman,
and between your offspring and hers;
he will crush your head,
and you will strike his heel."

Suddenly the child finds she has grown up; looks at herself awkwardly in the mirror, and sees the elder sister she always wanted to be like; but mourns the loss of the little girl she was. Self-awareness becomes self-consciousness – and becomes self-doubt or sometimes worse.

C S Lewis has an Eve-like character called the Green Woman, in his sci-fi novel *Perelandra*, who is offered a mirror by her tempter. He hopes that she will become, not innocently and simply herself, but a character in her own commentary on herself; that her mind will become a theatre in which her new reflected notion of herself holds the stage. It is a trap we in our world are all in.

The word 'paradise' originally meant an enclosed garden in the Middle East where the harsh realities of the desert and danger could be kept locked out. Now we are on the other side of the gate. The story of the Fall itself cannot – obviously – be history in the way that the later stories of the Patriarchs could be. Perhaps it is best seen as a projection backwards seeking to explain and understand this uncomfortable state in which we find ourselves in which what can go wrong does go wrong – and yet we know what 'wrong' means, and that there is a 'right' as well. Or, as St Paul described it, 'what I want to do I do not do, but what I hate I do.'

(Romans 7:15) And wherever we look, we can always look at ourselves so looking, and so on into an infinity of reflections.

So there is no simple naming now, but the whole package of shaming and blaming – the human condition that we know.

We have to face the truth about ourselves. But it also the truth that there is to be another garden, in Gethsemane, where a second Adam will take the blame on himself and this time God's will shall be done – and his kingdom shall come. And because of that there will be a garden too, one day, that will be Paradise Restored.

But if this is to be our story, we must live the story, not just look at it – in the mirror. Back through the looking glass we must go, and face the world from the right side on, and ourselves as we really are.

Lord God of no illusion
Help me to see myself again as you see me
In all simplicity
And give me the courage to break the glass
Of the mirrored maze that constrains me
In the prison of my own reflections
So I may become again, still adult, your child.

WEDNESDAY

The Covenant with Noah

Genesis 9.8-16

Then God said to Noah and to his sons with him: "I now establish my covenant with you and with your descendants after you and with every living creature that was with you – the birds, the livestock and all the wild animals, all those that came out of the ark with you – every living creature on earth. I establish my covenant with you: Never again will all life be cut off by the waters of a flood; never again will there be a flood to destroy the earth."

And God said, "This is the sign of the covenant I am making between me and you and every living creature with you, a covenant for all generations to come: I have set my rainbow in the clouds, and it will be the sign of the covenant between me and the earth. Whenever I bring clouds over the earth and the rainbow appears in the clouds, I will remember my covenant between me and you and all living creatures of every kind. Never again will the waters become a flood to destroy all life. Whenever the rainbow appears in the clouds, I will see it and remember the everlasting covenant between God and all living creatures of every kind on the earth."

Flooding became something very personal for us in January 2005, when our city suddenly found itself awash. The dramatic anguish of the high waters has now given way to the reality of long-term dislocation and a thousand smaller stories of turmoil and tragedy.

There is community in distress. The first donation to one of our flood-stricken churches came from Boscastle, recently flooded itself. Our own thoughts turned to the tsunami-stricken peoples of South East Asia. But that does not answer the big question of why there should be such distress in the first place. Our instinctive demand to be able to control the waters (better flood defences, better warnings) is undercut by the remembrance

that the largest cause of the extreme weather is our own actions bringing on global warming: our own fall leading to our own flood. But even that is cold comfort of an answer: a divine 'told you so' perhaps, as we are left to our fate.

But the flood is not the end. Noah's story stands for that bit of us which has not completely let go of God, and the discovery that God has not let go of us either.

The sign of the rainbow is an elusive one: it is real, but intangible; always just out of reach, but always coming back to surprise us. At a symbolic level it is a powerful response to those who see our faith as having nothing to say in the face of catastrophe. It is a pointer of promise within nature itself that 'red in tooth and claw' or 'blind evolution' are not the last words about it. Listen; look up; the story is not over yet.

> *Fear not, for I have redeemed you;*
> *I have summoned you by name; you are mine.*
> *When you pass through the waters, I will be with you;*
> *and when you pass through the rivers,*
> *they will not sweep over you.*
> (Isaiah 43:1-2)

To our fallen eyes, creation can seem also fallen and purposeless; but to faith it is God's handiwork still and carries his stamp, so that suddenly, in the rainbow, even in the rain, it can shine out with what Hopkins called a 'dearest freshness deep down things'.* And one day there will be another covenant in the waters of baptism that will be the sign and seal of our new creation in Christ.

 Today [the Epiphany celebration of the Baptism of Christ] the Holy Spirit hovers over the waters in the likeness of a dove. A dove announced to Noah that the flood had disappeared from the earth; so now a dove is to reveal that the world's shipwreck is at an end for ever. The sign is no longer an olive-shoot of the old stock: instead the Spirit pours out on Christ's head the full richness of a new anointing by the Father.
Peter Chysologus*

WEEK 1 THURSDAY

The Promise to Abraham

Genesis 22.9-18

When they reached the place God had told him about, Abraham built an altar there and arranged the wood on it. He bound his son Isaac and laid him on the altar, on top of the wood. Then he reached out his hand and took the knife to slay his son. But the angel of the Lord called out to him from heaven, "Abraham! Abraham!"

"Here I am," he replied.

"Do not lay a hand on the boy," he said. "Do not do anything to him. Now I know that you fear God, because you have not withheld from me your son, your only son."

Abraham looked up and there in a thicket he saw a ram caught by its horns.

He went over and took the ram and sacrificed it as a burnt offering instead of his son. So Abraham called that place The Lord Will Provide. And to this day it is said, "On the mountain of the Lord it will be provided."

The angel of the Lord called to Abraham from heaven a second time and said, "I swear by myself, declares the Lord, that because you have done this and have not withheld your son, your only son, I will surely bless you and make your descendants as numerous as the stars in the sky and as the sand on the seashore. Your descendants will take possession of the cities of their enemies, and through your offspring all nations on earth will be blessed, because you have obeyed me."

As a boy I sang in Britten's *War Requiem* with the Hallé orchestra. I can remember vividly the horror of the words interpolated there into the biblical text from Wilfred Owen's poetry: *But the old man would not so, but slew his son, – and half the seed of Europe, one by one.** At the heart of today's reading is the realization that God's mercy can triumph over his justice – a foundation stone of the great Abrahamic religions; but how hard we find it to follow that example, unmerciful servants that we are.

Setting aside our own vengeance, even when it is just, is though one of the most important things we can do to help bring in the kingdom of God.

Just as creation around us is ambivalent in the glimpse it gives us of God's goodness, so I suspect most of us find the people around us ambivalent as well, sometimes filling our hearts with joy and pride and wonder; sometimes disgusting and depressing us; and sometimes both in the same person.

This ambivalence can tempt us to give up on others and go it alone, either individually, or as a group. But we are made to be together. Other people, like nature, are a pointer of promise to us and a responsibility laid on us, and we are called to bless them as they bless us.

What might it mean for you or me to be a blessing to the people around us, now? To individuals; to nations; to the generations which will follow us? And, looking back to yesterday, how can we bless the land too, which so blesses us?

Holding our own blessing of others in harness with our receiving of God's blessing on us is important. Without it, for instance, the promise to Abraham of a land can become a dark one, and historically has been so. For 'cities of their enemies' read 'towns of the Palestinians' for example. We need to work together for a future that is blessing for all, and avoid the tempting shortcuts of sectarianism.

That Abraham's promise is inherited by three of today's world faiths is a good starting point. When I was last in Israel I met Riad again, a former chief of the British Tourist Police, Palestinian, Muslim, and tour guide extraordinaire. As we got to know each other better we talked religion – and found a common identity under Abraham as Friends of God. It isn't a bad place to start.

Blessed are you Lord God, King of the Universe
The one God, all-merciful
Friend of Abraham, Friend of Sinner.
Blessed are you, my brothers and sisters,
And blessed am I because of you.
The peace of the promise be with you all.

The Dream of Jacob

Genesis 28.10-17

Jacob left Beersheba and set out for Haran. When he reached a certain place, he stopped for the night because the sun had set. Taking one of the stones there, he put it under his head and lay down to sleep. He had a dream in which he saw a stairway resting on the earth, with its top reaching to heaven, and the angels of God were ascending and descending on it. There above it stood the Lord, and he said: "I am the Lord, the God of your father Abraham and the God of Isaac. I will give you and your descendants the land on which you are lying. Your descendants will be like the dust of the earth, and you will spread out to the west and to the east, to the north and to the south. All peoples on earth will be blessed through you and your offspring. I am with you and will watch over you wherever you go, and I will bring you back to this land. I will not leave you until I have done what I have promised you."

When Jacob awoke from his sleep, he thought, "Surely the Lord is in this place, and I was not aware of it." He was afraid and said, "How awesome is this place! This is none other than the house of God; this is the gate of heaven."

There is something very special about being able to crawl out of bed into my cathedral stall early in the morning to share in the prayer of the ages. T S Eliot wrote of a place 'where prayer has been valid';* others speak of Iona and Lindisfarne as places where the veil seems thin between this world and eternity; and there will have been places that have been special for you as well.

Noah's rainbow and Abraham's descendants have given us two pointers of promise in nature and in people: here is another, Jacob's ladder, reminding us that *places* too can be sacraments of God's presence.

They come in many shapes and sizes – but amongst them let me dwell for a moment on our familiar parish churches, where emblazoned over the door or in the roof, as in my old parish of Banbury, we may well find a text proclaiming just as Jacob did that, 'This is none other than the house of God, the gate of heaven.'

There and elsewhere, I used to leave the door of my church open whenever I was around, and someone nearly always came in: to find an oasis, look at the history, be inquisitive, pray. Many people, in fact, seem to prefer to be in church on their own rather than at a service, which says something about the times we live in, or our services, or both!

So for all our rhetoric about the church being the people not the building, buildings and places matter. Let me go back to those quiet moments early in the morning in the cathedral. I am no twister like Jacob, I hope, but I would blush to give you a blow-by-blow stream-of-consciousness account of everything that goes through my mind when I am supposed to be praying. Now that wouldn't be true of you of course … but here is hope for the majority of us whose motives are always mixed and prayer a

mixed bag of meanderings: we are there. We have taken the trouble to up stumps and get to a place where prayer has been valid – a church, a mountain, a chair in the corner (or underneath a skirt pulled over our head, which is how Susannah Wesley escaped the family). And once we are there, God, alarmingly incarnate in space and time, is there as well, and the wrestling match begins.

Getting it wrong, running away,
Painting our predicament in bold poster colours:
We find that you are there to surprise us,
Chortling quietly at our contortions.
The whole world of creation is yours,
The whole pile of people who inhabit it,
And there, round a corner, in a garden,
On the top of a bus
Is a ladder to heaven.

SATURDAY

The Law of Moses

Deuteronomy 6.1-9

These are the commands, decrees and laws the Lord your God directed me to teach you to observe in the land that you are crossing the Jordan to possess, so that you, your children and their children after them may fear the Lord your God as long as you live by keeping all his decrees and commands that I give you, and so that you may enjoy long life. Hear, O Israel, and be careful to obey so that it may go well with you and that you may increase greatly in a land flowing with milk and honey, just as the Lord, the God of your fathers, promised you.

Hear, O Israel: The Lord our God, the Lord is one. Love the Lord your God with all your heart and with all your soul and with all your strength. These commandments that I give you today are to be upon your hearts. Impress them on your children. Talk about them when you sit at home and when you walk along the road, when you lie down and when you get up. Tie them as symbols on your hands and bind them on your foreheads. Write them on the door-frames of your houses and on your gates.

I really am a bit of a twit. We were on a pilgrimage in Israel, and I was intrigued by some little boxes on the door frames. Secret surveillance? Electronic gadgetry? How embarrassed I was when I was politely referred to Deuteronomy 6.

In the boxes of course were tiny scrolls containing the commandments, the hotel keen to keep the forms of religion, even if life on the other side of the door might be spectacularly secular.

Now I was brought up in a vicarage household, but of the old high-to-middle variety where overt religion and daily life often felt more comfortable with the door shut between them.

Opening up that door is a life's work for most of us. For me, it has come in stages, with many still to come. One of them was after several years of ministry when I had something of an 'experience' and the Bible I had read and studied for many years seemed to leap off the page.

It wasn't about suddenly finding rules to live by or proof texts for my faith, but simply that the 'that' of the scriptures was the same as the 'this' of now, or better – a lively conversation began between the two that sometimes I managed to overhear.

This, I suppose, is what Moses was about, rather than the formalism of little boxes on doorframes. It could feel like the demand, or even threat, of law; but out of my own experience, I read it as another pointer of promise. Just as God is there to be found in creation, in other people, in places of prayer, so also he is there in the scriptures, and there in a way which relates to our everyday life.

And all this is BC – Before Christ. John V Taylor in his classic book *The Christ-like God** makes the point that what we know of God through Christ is true of God, full stop. Incarnation, revealing himself in the things of this world, is a fundamental part of who God is, and while it is in Christ that our salvation is revealed and assured, it is the same Christ-like God who was with us before Jesus' day and is with us now.

So, at the end of this first week of Advent, watch for the Christ who has come and will come – and breathe in his strength and his joy for today.

 O Lord our God,
make us watchful and keep us faithful
as we await the coming of your Son our Lord;
that, when he shall appear,
he may not find us sleeping in sin
but active in his service
and joyful in his praise;
through Jesus Christ our Lord. Amen.
Post-Communion Collect, Advent 1*

Taking Time Together

Set up an Advent wreath on a table in middle of the group. Dim the lights and wait quietly for a while. Then light the first of the candles with some appropriate words (perhaps the prayer I printed under Sunday), and as you look at the light reflect on how you have glimpsed something of God's promise. Each group member could light a small candle to stand for their glimpses, and could if they wished say something about them.

Put a symbolic object on the table for each of Noah, Abraham, Jacob and Moses. As each object is placed ask someone to read the Bible passage that was set for that patriarch's day. If possible, that person could have been asked to do so homework about 'their' patriarch, which they could share with the group. Talk together about ways in which the experiences of the patriarchs and our own lives match up.

How can the church community do more to share its stories of encouragement and challenge with one another? What actions or events could enable and symbolise this?

Make sure you leave a good space of time at the end to pray, and in particular to be quiet together, listening to God: it's easy to let this get crowded out! One way to 'hold' the space, particularly if you aren't used to being quiet together, is to choose an appropriate piece of music to play quietly in the background. I like John Tavener's 'The Lamb'. One of you needs to take responsibility for beginning and ending the time of quiet. The ending could appropriately include saying the Lord's Prayer and Grace together, and then extinguishing the candle.

SECOND SUNDAY IN ADVENT

The Prophets – alarm calls from God

Blessed are you, Sovereign Lord, just and true,
to you be praise and glory for ever!
Of old you spoke by the mouth of your prophets
but in our days you speak through your Son
whom you have appointed the heir of all things.
Grant us, your people, to walk in his light
that we may be found ready and watching
when he comes again in glory and judgement;
for you are our light and our salvation.
Blessed be God for ever.*

Over the last week we have seen that pointers to God's promise are still shining in creation around us: in human society and our own families, in special places and the sacred scriptures.

These signs are shot through with ambiguity, though, threat as well as promise. So God's work of redemption does not stop with these uncertain signs from deep history. Our down-to-earth deity,

working towards the definitive moment of the incarnation, seems to begin a struggle, a pregnancy to bring the Word to us.

The second Advent candle is for the prophets. Their oracles strike me as the pains of that pregnancy, real and sharp, but still not fully formed; urgent but not yet at full term. They are Advent's main course, at the heart of its spirituality. We can still receive them as signals, a series of alarm calls, to wake us up to God's word today, hindered runners that we are.

MONDAY

Darkness into light

Isaiah 9.2-7

The people walking in darkness have seen a great light; on those living in the land of the shadow of death a light has dawned. You have enlarged the nation and increased their joy; they rejoice before you as people rejoice at the harvest, as men rejoice when dividing the plunder. For as in the day of Midian's defeat, you have shattered the yoke that burdens them, the bar across their shoulders, the rod of their oppressor. Every warrior's boot used in battle and every garment rolled in blood will be destined for burning, will be fuel for the fire. For to us a child is born, to us a son is given, and the government will be on his shoulders. And he will be called Wonderful Counsellor, Mighty God, Everlasting Father, Prince of Peace. Of the increase of his government and peace there will be no end. He will reign on David's throne and over his kingdom, establishing and upholding it with justice and righteousness from that time on and for ever. The zeal of the Lord Almighty will accomplish this.

Isaiah prophesied seven centuries before Christ, not in the legendary world of Abraham and Moses but in the age of historical empires. The year Isaiah had his great vision and commission in the Temple (Isa. 6) was the year Ahaz came to the throne in Jerusalem. The terrifyingly named Tiglath Pileser III ruled the Assyrian Empire, and had devastated Galilee and the north. Was this to be the fate of Judah, or would God act to save them?

This was the shadow of death that hung over the people: the warrior's boot and the bloodstained clothes of the dead. As I write in July 2005 the acrid smell of terrorist bombings in London hangs in the air, and a generation that has taken freedom for granted is having to ask itself what that word is really going to mean for us and how it is to be won and held.

The question in our Advent journey is much the same. Living this side of Christmas, we take Christ for granted: but how is his kingdom actually going to come among us? How do the great promises to the patriarchs translate into historical reality?

Isaiah's prophecy brings a possibility and a problem. The possibility is that the tide of history will turn. The problem is that it might only be that, and that what Isaiah calls joy will in fact only be happiness – the good feeling when happenstances go right – for a while. Isaiah's alarm call says reach higher. Joy is something else – the deep lightness of heart that comes when we know that whatever the happenstances, all will be well. It has its roots not so much in the past as in the future and draws life from them to bring extravagant hope into even the worst of history.

So where do your roots lie? I have enjoyed sharing in my family's search for its ancestry over recent years as the 'roots' bug has bitten us as it has so many others. But though a family tree the size of a wall is fascinating, and knowing my forebears came out of the Highlands north of Perth five hundred years ago gives me a sort of identity: is that it? Are we just the conditioned products of our pedigrees? And where the past has hurt us, is that also it: and we must live with the scars?

No, we have other roots we can draw on – and in them can be healing as well as hope. Some of the roots reach out to those who love us; and some forward in hope to the God who loves us too. We do though, face a choice. We can sit by the waters of Babylon and bemoan our exile, and embrace bitterness; or we can reach out our roots into the water, and live.

Where are you putting your roots out to, now?
In the aftershock of the bombing
Hope lies in the balance.
Will we turn to the wall
Fight fire with fire
Or find the way that builds freedom?
Raise the flood of your waters, Lord,
To touch the reaching of our roots,
And enlarge our joy.

WEEK **2** TUESDAY

A virgin shall conceive

Isaiah 7.10-15

Again the Lord spoke to Ahaz, "Ask the Lord your God for a sign, whether in the deepest depths or in the highest heights."

But Ahaz said, "I will not ask; I will not put the Lord to the test."

Then Isaiah said, "Hear now, you house of David! Is it not enough to try the patience of men? Will you try the patience of my God also? Therefore the Lord himself will give you a sign: The virgin will be with child and will give birth to a son, and will call him Immanuel. He will eat curds and honey when he knows enough to reject the wrong and choose the right, the land of the two kings you dread will be laid waste.

As Isaiah speaks, Jerusalem is under siege from the kings of Israel and Aram. 'Don't lose heart because of these two smouldering stubs,' he says (v.4) – but Ahaz does not find trusting God easy. His response to the threat will be to offer vassalage to Tiglath Pileser, and change the Temple cult to appease him (2 Kings 16). His reluctance to put God to the test is not a doctrinal nicety but a diplomat's nerves.

Faced with this dithering, God offers a dramatic alarm call indeed. By the time a child soon to be born is of age, he and the nation will be living off milk and honey. But don't be misled by echoes of the promised land. They will be living off milk and honey, the land's natural produce, because all the cultivated goods will have been wasted; not by Israel and Aram (they too will be devastated), but by Assyria.

This does not sound like the comforting promise of a Christmas Carol service! The heart of the prophetic word, as so often, is a call to a radical trust in the Lord God, which is set in a dangerous tension with both the political process and a pluralist approach to religion.

This is both uncomfortable and contemporary. What does it mean to be a loyal believer today, and also a loyal citizen of a civil state and in particular of a pluralist one? Where do we stand?

What about the suicide bomber, the province that separates itself, the creationist who opposes evolution taught in schools ... Are they over the top? Or if we say that, are we being like Ahaz and deserting a simple trust in God? 'The government will be on his shoulders,' we read yesterday, but the media pundit asks whether 'ancient belief systems and modern government can find common ground.'*

So is the thrill that runs down our spine at the Carol Service when we hear the prophecy of Immanuel just a childish thing that we must put away as we struggle with hard reality?

No – but we have to receive the sign the right way. It is a sign that God is completely committed to our history and fully engaged with it. Yes, there is the comforting promise of a birth. But it is the birth of a child that will grow up – to some purpose. Will we let him?

Ann Lewin has a poem called 'Incarnation' which faces just this issue. Let me quote the beginning (and hope you search out the rest), as a way of helping you think just how much your own picture of the King and the Kingdom is kept at arm's length from the difficult decisions of political process.

He's grown, that Baby.
Not that most people have noticed.
He still looks the same,
Lying there in the straw, with
Animals and shepherds looking on.
He's safe there, locked in that moment
Where time met eternity.

Reality of course is different ... *

WEDNESDAY

Out of Bethlehem

Micah 5.2-5

"But you, Bethlehem Ephrathah,
though you are small among the clans
of Judah,
out of you will come for me
one who will be ruler over Israel,
whose origins are from of old,
from ancient times."
Therefore Israel will be abandoned
until the time when she who is in labour
gives birth

and the rest of his brothers return
to join the Israelites.
He will stand and shepherd his flock
in the strength of the Lord,
in the majesty of the name of the Lord
his God.
And they will live securely, for then his
greatness
will reach to the ends of the earth.
And he will be their peace.

So how small is yesterday's heavy work making you feel? Micah was a contemporary of Isaiah and the same background and themes are there in this prophecy – the abandonment of the land, a birth marking the time, a new age to come.

The tone, though, is different. Isaiah can be overwhelming, baroque, a major prophet in every sense of the world. He was, according to tradition, of royal blood, and the city is his stage.

Enter Micah of Moresheth: a younger man, from the countryside, direct enough in his prophecy but lyrical where Isaiah is epic. It seems appropriate that he should be the one not just to grasp, as Isaiah did,

that a great messianic Son would be born, but that with God it is human weakness that is most easily the channel of divine strength.

It is, of course, a Davidic theme, but one easily forgotten as memories of the shepherd boy were overlain by the annals of his kingship. Micah brings back the shepherd theme, an old metaphor for kingship evocatively recalled: the Son of David will watch over Israel as once David did his flock. As alarms go, this one is quieter, but just as insistent.

Micah's insight is that God's concern with the great sweep of history is mediated through small things. With the tincture 'for thy sake', as George Herbert puts it, 'nothing can be too mean';* and however complex and tragic the world around us our tiny part of the story is still of ultimate significance and can be used by God to effect.

I was struggling with this recently, and wondering where on earth my own vocation lay. (One needs a rather nuanced definition of vocation to cover the work of archdeacons, called the 'Rottweilers of the Church' by P. D. James in one of her thrillers.*) Then Rick Warren's book *The Purpose Driven Life* (subtitle *What on earth am I here for?*) turned my attention to Acts 13.36: 'David served God's purpose in his generation.'* If you're called David, it has to grab you. The simple message is that our calling is to be faithful where we are: and see what happens. And since not just David but the Son of David, Son of Man, Son of God is holding the shepherd's staff, a great deal indeed can happen if we let it.

Sometimes I wish that I might do
Just one grand deed and die,
And by that one grand deed reach up
To meet God in the sky.
But such is not Thy way, O God,
Not such is Thy decree,
But deed by deed, and tear by tear,
Our souls must climb to Thee.
G. A. Studdart-Kennedy*

THURSDAY

The Branch of David

Jeremiah 23.1-8

"Woe to the shepherds who are destroying and scattering the sheep of my pasture!" declares the Lord. Therefore this is what the Lord, the God of Israel, says to the shepherds who tend my people: "Because you have scattered my flock and driven them away and have not bestowed care on them, I will bestow punishment on you for the evil you have done," declares the Lord. "I myself will gather the remnant of my flock out of all the countries where I have driven them and will bring them back to their pasture, where they will be fruitful and increase in number. I will place shepherds over them who will tend them, and they will no longer be afraid or terrified, nor will any be missing," declares the Lord.

"The days are coming," declares the Lord,

"when I will raise up to David a righteous Branch,
a King who will reign wisely
and do what is just and right in the land.
In his days Judah will be saved
and Israel will live in safety.
This is the name by which he will be called:
The Lord Our Righteousness.

"So then, the days are coming," declares the Lord, "when people will no longer say, 'As surely as the Lord lives, who brought the Israelites up out of Egypt,' but they will say, 'As surely as the Lord lives, who brought the descendants of Israel up out of the land of the north and out of all the countries where he had banished them.' Then they will live in their own land."

A turn of the page, and time has moved on 150 years or so from our last reading into the world of Judah's last kings, just before their exile in Babylon. (Assyria itself has now been over-run.)

The promise of a second Davidic shepherd-king, a Branch of Jesse's tree, is still fresh, though, on the lips of the prophets. Such a long-term hope could easily lead to a sort of passive pietism; but Jeremiah is too much of a politician himself to leave it at that. The Lord gathers the people; but he appoints others to be shepherds under him who have very real responsibilities and will be held to account for them.

The challenging target for these under-shepherds is that none of the flock will go missing. Put together the inseparability of faith and society, and God's way of using not just great leaders but small players like you and me, and suddenly we ourselves are in the world of targets and accountability. Then the alarm call. It's not one that always sits easily with us. I am getting some very mixed comments as we find ourselves moving into the world of appraisal for parish clergy, for instance! But, with appropriate caveats, I'm not sure it's a move we should be resisting. There is important work to be done for God, and many of the opportunities lie in our hands. Some of the resistance feels like excuse-making.

The caveats, though, are important ones, and three of them are in today's passage. First, the work is God's before it is ours, he is active in it, and we need to look to him and trust him for it together. We may be significant, but we are still small. Second, since God's whole purpose is the safety of his sheep, we have no business conducting his in ways which scatter the flock. His reign is wise and just, and our actions must be the same. Third, this is a long-term project and we should not demand short-term fixes. 'The days' that are coming are the end-times, not the year end.

I've come at those principles with full-time Christian workers in mind: but come to think of it, aren't we all FTCW's,* and don't the same principles apply in all the work we do?

Grant, I may not like a puddle lie
In a corrupt security
Where, if a traveller water crave,
He finds it dead, and in a grave.
But as this restless vocal spring
All day and night doth run and sing,
And though here born, yet is acquainted
Elsewhere, and flowing keeps untainted;
So let me all my busy age
In thy free services engage.
Henry Vaughan*

The Spirit of the Lord

Isaiah 61.1-3

The Spirit of the Sovereign Lord is on me, because the Lord has anointed me to preach good news to the poor. He has sent me to bind up the broken-hearted, to proclaim freedom for the captives and release from darkness for the prisoners, to proclaim the year of the Lord's favour and the day of vengeance of our God, to comfort all who mourn, and provide for those who grieve in Zion – to bestow on them a crown of beauty instead of ashes,
the oil of gladness instead of mourning,
and a garment of praise instead of a spirit of despair.
They will be called oaks of right-eousness,
a planting of the Lord
for the display of his splendour.

I'm not sure, after all, that yesterday left us feeling any less challenged. The prophetic blast is insistent and does not let us rest; but it does not easily translate into a course of action that we can do and docket, and then rest again. That, of course, is by intention. And the answer we are driven to is equally by intention. Only the Spirit of God can do these things.

Today's passage catapults us forward again another 50 years to a time soon after the fall of the Babylonian Empire as the people of Israel glimpse the possibility of a return from exile. Powerless themselves, they had learnt the surprising lesson that even a Persian prince, Cyrus, could be the agent of God. Now, in terms reminiscent of the Cyrus oracles and Servant Songs earlier in the book, Isaiah casts a vision of the Spirit-anointed Servant Messiah, which Christ himself will both claim (Luke 4.14-21) and fulfil.

One of the great themes and truths of the scriptures is that the same Spirit which hovered over the waters in creation and fills a man like Joshua, and which hovered over Christ at his baptism and filled him, is also poured out on us and fills us too.* The alarm call is sounding a note that will be vital for the story to come. Without the Spirit's breath the ashes will never glow.

Talk of the Spirit can lead us quickly to matters of inspiration and spiritual gifts; but we often over-separate the persons of the Trinity, and today's passage from Isaiah reminds us, as does of course the life of Christ, that at heart the work of the Spirit is all one with Christ's work of Redemption. The Spirit comes on us and in us not as an overlay on our humanity but to transform it. This, and only this, is why the command that nothing be lost can be fulfilled: because nothing is beyond God's redemption. Even death gives way to life.

In some of my own darkest days it has been this truth that has kept me going – and I have often turned to the powerfully moving words of George Matheson's hymn to express it:

O Love that wilt not let me go,
I rest my weary soul in thee:
I give thee back the life I owe,
That in thine ocean depths its flow
May richer, fuller, be.

O Light that followest all my way,
I yield my flickering torch to thee:
My heart restores its borrowed ray,
That in thy sunshine's blaze its day
May brighter, fairer be.

O Joy that seekest me through pain,
I cannot close my heart to thee:
I trace the rainbow through the rain,
And feel the promise is not vain
That morn shall tearless be.

O Cross that liftest up my head,
I dare not ask to fly from thee:
I lay in dust in life's glory dead,
And from the ground there blossoms red
Life that shall endless be. *

WEEK 2

SATURDAY

The Messenger to Come

Malachi 3.1

"See, I will send my messenger, who will prepare the way before me. Then suddenly the Lord you are seeking will come to his temple; the messenger of the covenant, whom you desire, will come," says the Lord Almighty.

So to the last of the Old Testament books and the last of the Old Testament prophets: Malachi, who writes in the 500's BC and looks forward across a gap of half a millennium to another messenger (which is what Malachi means in Hebrew). Did he know that during those 500 years 'there was no voice, nor any that answered,* until John the Baptist broke the silence?

There is a common, if gruesome, theory that a frog may be boiled in a pan of water and will not jump out – as long as the temperature is raised slowly enough. Worryingly, the theory is also applied to our own complacency in the face of say global warming.

The application I have in mind now, though, is different but equally worrying. Sometimes the church services I attend – no, be honest, lead – are very willing to settle for the echo of the Voice, and it requires an alarm call indeed to make the frogs jump out of the water and desire something more.

It's a risky strategy, and one for God to prompt not for us to plot; but when it happens the sense of Presence is potent. We started a regular Healing Service at our Cathedral recently, and standing at the altar while a beautiful Taizé chant was being sung, I found myself carried away into ad hoc counterpoint and vocalization – and a little bit of heaven.

The point of the story for now is that it whetted my appetite again for God's presence, and I hope it might whet yours. If the Lord is to come into his Temple, our desire is part of the plan. While the voice of the Lord was silent, also silent were the 'Quiet in the Land', like Simeon righteous and devout and 'waiting for the consolation of Israel'.* Their day will come.

So the end of this week and the onslaught of the prophets brings us to the great Advent theme of expectation: not taking the waiting out of wanting or the wanting out of waiting, but waiting with sometimes painful wanting, for the Birth, for the Advent, for the Lord who is to come.

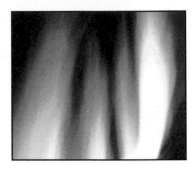

> *So light up the fire and let the flame burn,*
> *Open the door, let Jesus return.*
> *Take seeds of His Spirit, let the fruit grow,*
> *Tell the people of Jesus, let His love show.**

Lord, I'm afraid I'm becoming a frog,
Far too comfortable in my warming pond
To jump out and live.
So turn up the fire, Lord,
And wake me up
From my religious reverie.
Put a bit of the prophet in me,
A holy impatience with words that are empty
And deeds that are absent
(In me, Lord, in me),
And inflame my prayer
With tongues of flaming desire
To encounter you in your temple,
Lord of all liveliness, Lord of all Life.

STUDY NOTES FOR WEEK TWO

Taking Time Together

When the group has settled down and is catching up on the news, light two candles in your Advent wreath. You could use the 'Prophets' prayer I printed for this last Sunday. Invite each person to share some news (no interruptions or questions!) about whether for them God feels near or far away, is speaking or is silent. It's important not to make this a competition: we all have times of all of these, and they are all part of our journey. What we are doing here is supporting one another in saying 'how it is' before God.

I've called the prophets God's 'alarm calls'. Sometimes when God speaks to us it is gentle and reassuring. Sometimes, though, he wants to stir us up. Invite conversation about times when God has stirred you up in some way – it might have been a moving television programme, an encounter with someone in need, an illness, a challenge. What did it lead to? Is there more to be done?

Go on to ask whether there is anything that you believe God is trying to stir you up about as a church community? What should you be doing about that?

Have a number of stones ready. Think of them as stones that God is throwing at your windows to catch your attention! As you pray together, you can pick up a stone from the pile and put it by the candles, naming it for something you mentioned earlier as a prompt from God. 'This stone is for the Big Issue seller that I never know quite how to react to.' Music to listen to? Handel's 'Messiah' sets some of the prophetic texts we have been looking at.

WEEK 3

The Baptist – preparing the way

Blessed are you, Sovereign Lord, just and true:
to you be praise and glory for ever!
Your prophet John the Baptist was witness to the truth
as a burning and shining light.
May we your servants rejoice in his light,
and so be led to witness to him
who is the Lord of our coming Kingdom,
Jesus our Saviour and King of the ages.
Blessed be God for ever.*

Any day now, if you are reading this in season, and global warming being what it is, you'll be seeing the first snowdrops push through the soil, harbingers of spring. In the 'Narnia' books the breaking of the spell over the land shows as the first signs of thaw set in, and Father Christmas' sleigh is seen

again.* Not of course Christ (even if some do get confused!) but bringing *presents* that are signs of the *presence* to come.

The third Advent Candle is for John the Baptist, the fore-runner, the ice-breaker. It is time to move from long-term waiting to short-term preparation. You may well be decking your hall with holly this week, and loading the loft with presents and the larder with provisions. What will you deck your soul with, good Christian, and what good things has your Father in Heaven prepared for you to enjoy?

MONDAY

The Genealogy

Matthew 1.1-17

A record of the genealogy of Jesus Christ the son of David, the son of Abraham:
Abraham was the father of Isaac,
Isaac the father of Jacob,
Jacob the father of Judah and his brothers,
Judah the father of Perez and Zerah, whose mother was Tamar,
Perez the father of Hezron,
Hezron the father of Ram,
Ram the father of Amminadab,
Amminadab the father of Nahshon,
Nahshon the father of Salmon,
Salmon the father of Boaz, whose mother was Rahab,
Boaz the father of Obed, whose mother was Ruth,
Obed the father of Jesse,
and Jesse the father of King David.
David was the father of Solomon, whose mother had been Uriah's wife,
Solomon the father of Rehoboam,
Rehoboam the father of Abijah,
Abijah the father of Asa,
Asa the father of Jehoshaphat,
Jehoshaphat the father of Jehoram,
Jehoram the father of Uzziah,
Uzziah the father of Jotham,
Jotham the father of Ahaz,
Ahaz the father of Hezekiah,
Hezekiah the father of Manasseh,
Manasseh the father of Amon,
Amon the father of Josiah,
and Josiah the father of Jeconiah and his brothers
at the time of the exile to Babylon.
After the exile to Babylon:
Jeconiah was the father of Shealtiel,
Shealtiel the father of Zerubbabel,
Zerubbabel the father of Abiud,
Abiud the father of Eliakim,
Eliakim the father of Azor,
Azor the father of Zadok,
Zadok the father of Akim,
Akim the father of Eliud,
Eliud the father of Eleazar,
Eleazar the father of Matthan,
Matthan the father of Jacob,
and Jacob the father of Joseph, the husband of Mary, of whom was born Jesus, who is called Christ.
　Thus there were fourteen generations in all from Abraham to David, fourteen from David to the exile to Babylon, and fourteen from the exile to the Christ.

How would you feel if you suddenly discovered a whole book about the history of your family? Some old film was found recently from our neck of the woods. It showed crowds of ordinary folk in northern towns, and people were transfixed to see their great-grandparents strutting their stuff, not just names but living people.

Matthew's genealogy is not just names either. Behind each of them is a story, many known to us from the pages of the Old Testament, and Matthew is keen not to airbrush out the more colourful moments to do with women. Tamar, Rahab, Ruth and Uriah's wife would provide quite enough copy to keep a tabloid going for weeks. For Matthew they tie the history of the past to the story of his present – the equally potentially scandalous motherhood of Mary.

For us too it brings ancient history and modern times together. Here are people like us, with the same complicated relationships and compromised morality, still part of God's lineage and God's plan, just as we are when we come to know ourselves as brothers and sisters of Christ, children of God.

What do you think your part, however small, might be in preparing the way?

O Lord Jesus Christ,
who at your first coming sent your messenger
to prepare your way before you:
grant that the ministers and stewards of your mysteries
may likewise so prepare and make ready your way
by turning the hearts of the disobedient to the wisdom of the just,
that at your second coming to judge the world
we may be found an acceptable people in your sight;
for you are alive and reign with the Father
in the unity of the Holy Spirit,
one God, now and for ever. Amen.

Collect for the Third Sunday in Advent. *

TUESDAY

The Birth Foretold

Luke 1.5-25

In the time of Herod king of Judea there was a priest named Zechariah, who belonged to the priestly division of Abijah; his wife Elizabeth was also a descendant of Aaron. Both of them were upright in the sight of God, observing all the Lord's commandments and regulations blamelessly. But they had no children, because Elizabeth was barren; and they were both well on in years.

Once when Zechariah's division was on duty and he was serving as priest before God, he was chosen by lot, according to the custom of the priesthood, to go into the temple of the Lord and burn incense. And when the time for the burning of incense came, all the assembled worshippers were praying outside.

Then an angel of the Lord appeared to him, standing at the right side of the altar of incense. When Zechariah saw him, he was startled and was gripped with fear. But the angel said to him: "Do not be afraid, Zechariah; your prayer has been heard. Your wife Elizabeth will bear you a son, and you are to give him the name John. He will be a joy and delight to you, and many will rejoice because of his birth, for he will be great in the sight of the Lord. He is never to take wine or other fermented drink, and he will be filled with the Holy Spirit even from birth. Many of the people of Israel will he bring back to the Lord their God. And he will go on before the Lord, in the spirit and power of Elijah, to turn the hearts of the fathers to their children and the disobedient to the wisdom of the righteous – to make ready a people prepared for the Lord."

Zechariah asked the angel, "How can I be sure of this? I am an old man and my wife is well on in years."

The angel answered, "I am Gabriel. I stand in the presence of God, and I have been sent to speak to you and to tell you this good news. And now you will be silent and not able to speak until the day this happens, because you did not believe my words, which will come true at their proper time."

Meanwhile, the people were waiting for Zechariah and wondering why he stayed so long in the temple. When he came out, he could not speak to them. They realised he had seen a vision in the temple, for he kept making signs to them but remained unable to speak.

When his time of service was completed, he returned home. After this his wife Elizabeth became pregnant and for five months remained in seclusion. "The Lord has done this for me," she said. "In these days he has shown his favour and taken away my disgrace among the people."

God, our down-to-earth God, meets us where we are. For the story of how God breathed life back into his people, who better to turn to than Luke, the story-teller and historian *par excellence* of the New Testament.

Zechariah and Elizabeth were pillars of the religious life of their day, but the story suggests that there is something barren about their religion as well as their marriage. God brings new life to both. Zechariah enters the Holy of Holies, the once-in-a-lifetime pinnacle of the priestly ministry. It had long been empty, looted of its treasures, the sign of a now absentee landlord, to use the image of Jesus' parables. Suddenly, the Lord returns to his temple, an angel appears, his voice is heard again, and the old order is to be made new.

I mentioned earlier that I too grew up in a priestly family. But while we can be formed so far by our parents (and I am grateful for it), the fullness of the Spirit has to be found by each of us for ourselves – and I remember long wrestling matches in prayer as I tried to force God to come out from his hiding place.

Just as Zechariah had first to learn that this was God's work not his own – and was struck dumb to make sure – so for me when the Lord did come into his temple it was not in the security of my own tradition or the thrust of my own prayer. Instead it was outsider friends who prayed for me by night, when all my own resources were spent.

Is today's story an invitation to you to find some quiet place and listen for what God is preparing in you?

How strange to be told
that the church floor was too hard
for prayer.
But then I had never reckoned
that prayer might mean
that I was floored,
and set on quite a new foundation.

WEDNESDAY

The Visitation

Luke 1.39-45

At that time Mary got ready and hurried to a town in the hill country of Judea, where she entered Zechariah's home and greeted Elizabeth. When Elizabeth heard Mary's greeting, the baby leaped in her womb, and Elizabeth was filled with the Holy Spirit. In a loud voice she exclaimed: "Blessed are you among women, and blessed is the child you will bear! But why am I so favoured, that the mother of my Lord should come to me? As soon as the sound of your greeting reached my ears, the baby in my womb leaped for joy. Blessed is she who has believed that what the Lord has said to her will be accomplished!"

We encountered barrenness yesterday. God does act, but the ruin is a real one. Today's action takes place in Bethlehem or a town like it, in the Judaean hills. Go there now and you will find a barren place indeed, the buildings blasted by gunfire, the tourists only a trickle, the Christian population an echo of what it was.

The ruined buildings make me think of those often found in paintings of the Nativity. They are there because a legend had grown up that the Temple of Peace fell ruined on the very day that Christ was born, the old order giving way to the new. Can we read today's ruins as signs of new life as well as symbols of the desolation of the old?

What makes a difference for Elizabeth is the moving of the Holy Spirit in her. She is full, in her pregnancy, of the old sort of life that will always live under the shadow of death. She is filled, through God's grace, with the Holy Spirit which is the sign of a new sort of life from God.

The Spirit comes in the midst of the ruins, in the town, in the barrenness. We can legitimately say that this is precisely how it always comes, because its job is to give and renew life, not just decorate it.

That is why barrenness in the Bible is so often a prelude to birth: it is God's nature to work things that way.

What, though, when our barrenness seems for ever? Perhaps it is actual childlessness, perhaps the glass cage of a condition like M.E., or perhaps simple grinding poverty, or the frozen wasteland of the victim of abuse. What then?

See in the story how Elizabeth's joy comes from Mary's pregnancy, not her own. Later Anna, the lifelong widow, will feel the same effect.

Introspective by nature, I spend far too long looking in at myself, and can easily lose sight of God. When I minister to others it is probably more of a gift to me than to them because then I look out and look up and see the Spirit move.

At an individual level it is simply a fact that not all will find the fulfillment that they long for. But whoever said that everything had to stay at that level? We are made to be together, a family, a team. Making goals is just as important as scoring them. And perhaps helping others find fulfilment is, paradoxically, even more fulfilling than simply being fulfilled ourselves.

The Baptist is no bit player as fore-runner to the Messiah, and neither are you as his follower. Is there something you could do today for someone else, to prepare God's way, however small, however secret?

 Elizabeth is the first to hear Mary's voice, but John is the first to be aware of grace. Elizabeth hears with the ears of the body, but John leaps for joy at the meaning of the mystery ... The women speak the grace they have received, while the children are active in secret, unfolding the mystery of love with the help of their mothers, who prophesy by the spirit of their sons.
St Ambrose*

THURSDAY

The Magnificat

Luke 1.46-56

And Mary said:
"My soul glorifies the Lord
and my spirit rejoices in God my Saviour,
for he has been mindful
of the humble state of his servant.
From now on all generations will call me blessed,
for the Mighty One has done great things for me –
holy is his name.
His mercy extends to those who fear him,
from generation to generation.
He has performed mighty deeds with his arm;
he has scattered those who are proud in their inmost thoughts.
He has brought down rulers from their thrones
but has lifted up the humble.
He has filled the hungry with good things
but has sent the rich away empty.
He has helped his servant Israel,
remembering to be merciful
to Abraham and his descendants for ever,
even as he said to our fathers."

Mary stayed with Elizabeth for about three months and then returned home.

'Any woman could say it. For every one of them, God is in her child.' So says Varykino commenting on the 'Magnificat' in Pasternak's *Dr Zhivago*.* So although Mary sings out her song for a child beyond compare, Prince of Peace and Lord of Lords, she sings it out too for all of us, mother's children that we all are. It is Mary's humility that is the key here. Because of that she is representative of all mothers, none so lowly that they are beneath her, though none could claim a higher place. And because of that too, she is the proper human parent for the Saviour who humbles himself, who endows him with the human humility and obedience which can march so in step with the divine that with one united will he can accomplish the work of the Cross.

Luke tells us that Mary and Elizabeth were related, so that humanly Jesus and John were too. If so, we could dare to say that John shares in this family's human DNA of humility too. Certainly he later says and accepts that he must decrease and Jesus must increase, baptizes him with reluctance, and sees that he is not worthy enough to even untie his sandals.

It is in that humility, though, as in Christ's, that the power lies to challenge the rules of his time and dare to send the rich away empty while filling the poor with good things.

Remembrance Sunday happens to be close as I write, and while preparing to preach to the county on parade I ponder how universal a law this is, that true power is allied to true humility. Only when we know ourselves no more worthy before God than our enemy are we in a place to oppose the evil of our enemy without simply usurping his position and becoming evil ourselves.

This was of course Jesus' great temptation, to out-devil the devil, but in him we see perfectly combined the deepest humility, laying himself open to God's, the deepest strength, so that in the power of God he can change the world.

Perhaps today is a day to pray for the John figures of today and for all our own calls to be humble in preparing the way of the kingdom.

'To prepare the way' means to pray well; it means thinking humbly of oneself. We should take our lesson from John the Baptist. He pointed out clearly who he was; he humbled himself. He saw where his salvation lay. He understood that he was a lamp, and his fear was that it might be blown out by the wind of pride.
St Augustine*

FRIDAY

The Birth of the Baptist

Luke 1.57-66

When it was time for Elizabeth to have her baby, she gave birth to a son. Her neighbours and relatives heard that the Lord had shown her great mercy, and they shared her joy.

On the eighth day they came to circumcise the child, and they were going to name him after his father Zechariah, but his mother spoke up and said, "No! He is to be called John."

They said to her, "There is no-one among your relatives who has that name."

Then they made signs to his father, to find out what he would like to name the child. He asked for a writing tablet, and to everyone's astonishment he wrote, "His name is John." Immediately his mouth was opened and his tongue was loosed, and he began to speak, praising God. The neighbours were all filled with awe, and throughout the hill country of Judea people were talking about all these things. Everyone who heard this wondered about it, asking, "What then is this child going to be?" For the Lord's hand was with him.

At the heart of today's passage is the naming of John. There is nothing special, as far as I can see, about the name. It's as ordinary as mine, and probably yours. What is special about it is that it is the name chosen by God; and the need is for the actors in the story to let their choice follow his, to incarnate his truth. Until the choice is made the story is in suspense: when the sign is given, Zechariah's tongue is unlocked and the Spirit is too.

This passage reminds us that ordinary as we are, we are also in some sense known and named by God, and that discovering our identity in him is the key which will unlock our lives to be fruitful in and for him.

There is work for each of us here – but the passage makes my own thoughts turn to today's children, and especially to those brought for baptism. How are they going to become the people God is planning and preparing them to be? How will their potential be properly fulfilled, not just in consumer choice, but in Christ-like maturity?

I have lost count of the number of times I have held a child in my arms, said the words and poured the water, but the moment never fails to send a shiver down my spine. 'What then is this child going to be?' Praying extempore for the child a little later, it would often be strangely the child's name that seemed to open the door to some word from God for him or her, and my heart would yearn that all of God's promise would be fulfilled for them.

We are back to expectation again, that Christ will come in our lives now, and come one day with life in all its fullness. Perhaps you could pray today particularly for this in the lives of children you know, and for the critical work of the Church in passing on this hope of life to many children today. Is there something you could do this Christmas to prepare a way of faith for a child you know?

Words:
I've lived with them so long
That they seem to have a life of their own;
But like all of creation
They only echo right
When they say your Word after you,
Trembling with its truth,
Resonating with its righteousness.
Words:
They are like children,
Learning your language of love,
Then growing up
To speak it to others.

The Benedictus

Luke 1.67-80

His father Zechariah was filled with the Holy Spirit and prophesied:

"Praise be to the Lord, the God of Israel,
because he has come and has redeemed his people.
He has raised up a horn of salvation for us
in the house of his servant David
(as he said through his holy prophets of long ago),
salvation from our enemies
and from the hand of all who hate us –
to show mercy to our fathers
and to remember his holy covenant,
the oath he swore to our father Abraham:
to rescue us from the hand of our enemies,

°and to enable us to serve him without fear
in holiness and righteousness before him all our days.
And you, my child, will be called a prophet of the Most High;
for you will go on before the Lord to prepare the way for him,
to give his people the knowledge of salvation
through the forgiveness of their sins,
because of the tender mercy of our God,
by which the rising sun will come to us from heaven
to shine on those living in darkness
and in the shadow of death,
to guide our feet into the path of peace."

There are not many passages of Scripture or pieces of any sort of literature that can bear being read aloud in company every day of every week – but this is one of them, a fixture as it is in Anglican Morning Prayer. And what a morning canticle it makes! 'The dawn from on high will break upon us,' as my usual version has it, that will shine into our darkness and guide our steps in the way of peace.

This is not just a prayer for the atmospheric gloom of a mediaeval cathedral whose old lighting system was famously described by a former Dean as the only one in England that made the place darker when it was switched on. It is a prayer for the present work of our down-to-earth God in our everyday world of very real darkness and very real need for discerning choice.

This week has had a lot in it about expectation and expectancy – 'expecting' in the everyday sense of the world, and an attitude of mind and spirit that we are called to as the people of God. This sort of expectancy is sustained when we have a deep sureness that what we are expecting is going to really happen and really make a difference, and a difference that we really need. It is a sort of springtime in our spirit.

In a less religious sphere think how a family will strain every sinew to raise the money for a miracle cure, or how a resistance movement will risk everything for the sake of liberation to come. Then we are starting to get close to the call of John and Jesus to be part of the breaking in of a new sort of kingdom of healing and freedom.

Let me invite you as this week ends to think for a moment of the gap which lies between our excitement and expectancy at the call of Christ, and the way it was heard all those years ago. If we really do want to see light shine in our darkness, to see forgiveness and freedom, peace and prosperity – then now is the time to stoke up the fire of our faith again. Today as I write Archbishop Sentamu is being installed in York – with a name that means fire-stoker for the King. Let's join the awakening.

We give you thanks, O Lord, for these heavenly gifts;
kindle in us the fire of your Spirit
that when your Christ comes again
we may shine as lights before his face;
who is alive and reigns now and for ever. Amen.
Post-communion Collect for the Third Sunday in Advent.*

Taking Time Together

Three candles to light this week; and I think you might risk a bit of decoration! A new tradition, if that's not a contradiction in terms, has grown up of the Advent or Chrismon tree – using symbols of Christ and the like. Think Alpha and Omega, the Chi Rho, the Cross, a Lamb and Flag, star of David … Perhaps each group member could make one or two and bring them along, and then add them to the table with a prayer.

That should set the scene for a discussion of what getting ready for Christmas is feeling like, and in particular for how we can get ready for it as a festival of Christ, not just a family blow-out. No guilt trips, please – but you might pick up some good ideas and encouragement from each other.

How can our church help us take the festival out of the church building and into the homes and lives of the church people? One idea that works well is to make up a bag with a crib set in it, and books with Christmas stories and prayers – and pass it round so that the Holy Family spend each night in a different home before reaching church at Christmas. The Church Army promote it under the name *Posada* (see this coming Sunday's note). Is this something your group could set up now? A bit of action output is not a bad idea for groups like this – it helps them stop being talking shops.

In your prayer time, remember to 'take time' again. For meditative music, there's a magnificent Magnificat on Margaret Rizza's 'Fountain of Life' CD (Kevin Mayhew kmcd 10310). You could add your own words of praise to its accompaniment. A Taizé chant would work as well, or a song like Betty Pulkingham's 'Alleluia' (CMP29).

FOURTH SUNDAY IN ADVENT

The Birth – around Christ's crib

Blessed are you, Sovereign Lord, merciful and gentle:
to you be praise and glory for ever!
Your light has shone in our darkened world
through the child-bearing of blessed Mary;
grant that we who have seen your glory
may daily be renewed in your image
and prepared like her for the coming of your Son,
who is the Lord and Saviour of all.
Blessed be God for ever..*

The fourth candle is for Mary, waiting for the Birth. Christmas will come some time this week. (If it's before Sunday, you may like to use the page for Christmas Day when it does.) It's time to get the Crib Set out and make a focus for faith in the midst of the mistletoe.

It was St Francis who more or less invented the crib scene, setting up a life-sized one at Greccio in 1229, with a live ox and ass. In South America a real Mary and Joseph might call at your house at this time, making it their posada or inn for the night; and posada bags of colourful crib figures, story books and prayers now pass round the families of our own parishes, inviting all there to kneel by the crib and say a Christmas prayer. It's all part of taking faith out into the family, not just asking the family to go to church.*

During the coming week you are invited to think about each of the figures in turn, and about your own way of connecting with Christ, what your gift to him might be, and his to you.

MONDAY

Mary

Luke 1.26-38

In the sixth month, God sent the angel Gabriel to Nazareth, a town in Galilee, to a virgin pledged to be married to a man named Joseph, a descendant of David. The virgin's name was Mary. The angel went to her and said, "Greetings, you who are highly favoured! The Lord is with you."

Mary was greatly troubled at his words and wondered what kind of greeting this might be. But the angel said to her, "Do not be afraid, Mary, you have found favour with God. You will be with child and give birth to a son, and you are to give him the name Jesus. He will be great and will be called the Son of the Most High. The Lord God will give him the throne of his father David, and he will reign over the house of Jacob for ever; his kingdom will never end."

"How will this be," Mary asked the angel, "since I am a virgin?"

The angel answered, "The Holy Spirit will come upon you, and the power of the Most High will overshadow you. So the holy one to be born will be called the Son of God. Even Elizabeth your relative is going to have a child in her old age, and she who was said to be barren is in her sixth month. For nothing is impossible with God."

"I am the Lord's servant," Mary answered. "May it be to me as you have said." Then the angel left her.

Mary is generally portrayed as even more meek and mild than her son Jesus – but I'm not sure that's true. Look at the Bible stories again. Her response to the angel is quite as forthright as that of the prophets, and we see her naturally in company and often with something to say. It can be quite instructive to turn the pages and read, as it were, the *Gospel according to Mary* – and instructive too to remember that much of Luke's account can only have come from her lips.

So here is a woman who is not afraid to speak, to stand on equal terms even with an angel – even in a way with God, because God does not bring about the conception of

Christ by *force majeure* or a trick, like Zeus in the Greek myths, but with her willing consent. Deliberately and importantly, this is a decision freely entered into by both parties – and both give gifts of ultimate value to seal it and set it in motion: both give themselves.

> *Gift better than himself God doth not know;*
> *Gift better than his God no man can see.*
> *This gift doth here the giver given bestow;*
> *Gift to this gift let each receiver be.*
> *God is my gift, himself he freely gave me;*
> *God's gift am I, and none but God shall have me.**

This significance of gift exchange is worth recovering in an age when gifts have become commodities, glitzy on the outside but hollow within, things we don't really like, bought with money we don't really have, given to people we don't really care for.*

Here, by contrast, Mary and God bend towards each other, and accept each other with the deepest respect, as Fra Filippo Lippi so movingly painted it, if you have the chance to see his *Annunciation* in London's National Gallery.* There is no present but themselves, and the gifts are unconditional.

 Give your answer quickly, my Virgin. My Lady, speak the word which earth and heaven itself are waiting for. The very king and lord of all, 'he who desires your beauty', is eager for your assent, by which he proposes to save the world. You have pleased him by your silence: you will please him even more by your word.
St Bernard*

TUESDAY

Joseph

Matthew 1.18-25

This is how the birth of Jesus Christ came about: His mother Mary was pledged to be married to Joseph, but before they came together, she was found to be with child through the Holy Spirit. Because Joseph her husband was a righteous man and did not want to expose her to public disgrace, he had in mind to divorce her quietly.

But after he had considered this, an angel of the Lord appeared to him in a dream and said, "Joseph son of David, do not be afraid to take Mary home as your wife, because what is conceived in her is from the Holy Spirit. She will give birth to a son, and you are to give him the name Jesus, because he will save his people from their sins."

All this took place to fulfil what the Lord had said through the prophet: "The virgin will be with child and will give birth to a son, and they will call him Immanuel" – which means, "God with us."

When Joseph woke up, he did what the angel of the Lord had commanded him and took Mary home as his wife. But he had no union with her until she gave birth to a son. And he gave him the name Jesus.

Not everyone is as comfortable in company as Mary, or as quick to find something to say. Joseph has it in mind to divorce Mary *quietly*, and he could be the archetype of the strong but silent, righteous yet reserved countryman that I have met so often in Cumbria. In all the gospels he does not say a word. The gift he gives is one of silent support to Mary, and obedience to God.

He reminds me too of the lakes near where I live, surrounded by crowds of visitors and the bustle of the tourist business, but nevertheless standing deep and still, disturbed only by the wind-driven waves and the wakes of water-craft.

The news of Mary's pregnancy cuts a wake in what must have been Joseph's honest expectations. How easy it would have been to react with anger, to beat Mary or abandon her. How easy too for us to react roughly when our peace is put out in this season of stress, and hopes too often unfulfilled.

Joseph has to draw deep on his reserves. The angel addresses him as son of David. The earlier genealogy has prepared us for this, and Joseph now finds strength in the acknowledgment of an ancestry that he must have been proud to recite. He finds strength too in his spirituality, and gives the angelic dream due assent. He also finds strength in the scriptures, which as a righteous man he would have read and remembered. And in this strength he is able to obey God's will, and let Mary's boat float on his water.

Joseph teaches us that beneath and beyond the bustle of Christmas the deep peace of the Prince of Peace is there to be found, if we choose to draw on it, rather than return fire when fortune's slings and arrows wound us, as sooner or later they always do.

The still surface of the lake reflects back the hills around it in a wonderful harmony. Part of our gift to others this Christmas can be to listen to them carefully, reflect back to them thoughtfully, and live with them peacefully – a silent support.

Deep peace of the Running Wave to you.
Deep peace of the Flowing Air to you.
Deep peace of the Quiet Earth to you.
Deep peace of the Shining Stars to you.
Deep peace of the Son of Peace to you.
Celtic Benediction*

Caesar

Luke 2.1-5

In those days Caesar Augustus issued a decree that a census should be taken of the entire Roman world. (This was the first census that took place while Quirinius was governor of Syria.) And everyone went to his own town to register.

So Joseph also went up from the town of Nazareth in Galilee to Judea, to Bethlehem the town of David, because he belonged to the house and line of David. He went there to register with Mary, who was pledged to be married to him and was expecting a child.

Another man strides out onto the stage – Caesar Augustus, Emperor of Rome. His birth like that of Jesus was also (according to Suetonius) attended by magi from the east. He came to be called Saviour, Lord, King of the world, worshipped as a God. He makes quite a contrast to Joseph. The most obvious thing, though, about him, from the perspective of our crib set, is that like T. S. Eliot's mystery cat Macavity, he isn't there, even though without his edict none of this would have come to pass.

An interesting insight in passing is that according to strict Roman law, Joseph should not have been there either, since the place of registration was where one held property. It is a concession to Jewish custom that takes Joseph rather to the place where his lineage held its land, a matter of people rather than possessions.

Augustus offers power, prestige and property – but it is Joseph who offers the gift of his presence.

Making the effort to be there, to be one of the family, is part of what Christmas is about, most obviously the family of our kin, but I hope also the family of our church. It can be a costly affair.

I remember walking to church one morning in a Midlands parish and seeing pass what seemed to be car after car carrying single men, laden with large presents for children to whom they themselves were no longer normally present. But no gift however big can stand proxy for that presence – as they themselves will have sadly known, as they lived out the consequences of their broken relationships; and yet to stay away, give nothing, would be even worse.

It can be costly too when we are able to be present, but when the relationships are not easy, or when we feel the call to be with the family of our faith, but the other members of the family of our home do not.

Perhaps it is important not to impose a counsel of perfection on ourselves or others here. Just managing to be there, in a tolerable temper, may be gift enough! The way Joseph is painted in Nativities can give us heart. Especially in the earlier ones the artists seem to have rather assumed that he was a bit on the edge, so in della Francesca's painting in the National Gallery you'll see him sitting, for instance, on his saddle, rubbing his feet still sore from leading Mary on the journey, while excited shepherds try to catch his attention. Giotto shows him having a quiet snooze, while van Soest has him on hands and knees blowing at the fire.* There is hope for the male of the species yet! But male or female, just being there, whether we feel we fit or not, is a gift we can give.

There I am Lord –
Well, part of me anyway –
Crumpled in my comfy chair
After the Christmas service marathon.
Thank you – for the family who love me back to life.
Thank you – that, when I finally surface,
The more I give, the more I gain.

THURSDAY

The Christ-child

Luke 2.6-7
While they were there, the time came for the baby to be born, and she gave birth to her firstborn, a son. She wrapped him in cloths and placed him in a manger, because there was no room for them in the inn.

The life of a new-born baby is frighteningly fragile. The baby Jesus lies in his manger at the centre of our crib scene, dwarfed by the adults around him. He is utterly dependent on them – but see how he captivates their gaze. Like any baby, his powerlessness has the power to unlock hearts and elicit love from even the hardest of cases.

Christ's gift to us at Christmas is one of love, and a sort of love that goes beyond our normal love-giving, the willing unlocking of our own hearts, offering affection, preferring the other. This is also God's love for us – but his goes deeper. The helpless child, at this early stage, does not so much offer let alone understand its own love; it elicits ours. God not only gives us his own love, he gives us our ability to love, love itself, so that we can become as he is.

When Francis built the first crib at Greccio, Mass was said over the manger, and in paintings which came afterwards the manger can often take on the form of an altar. A close connection is being made between Christ's self-offering in birth and his self-offering on the Cross, and so also in the Eucharist, a gift of love which spends itself for the beloved.

Drained is love in making full;
Bound in setting others free;
Poor in making many rich;
Weak in giving power to be.*

I said that the hardest of hearts can be unlocked before such love –
but not always. Not only are God and the good rejected, but
children in their innocence are abused. If we have to face these
unpalatable truths, it was to face them too that Christ was born.
Austin Farrer reminds us that our fixation on power, our feel for it
and our fear of it, has made it impossible for us to know the love
of God as Lord without layering it over with the products of our
own power-play. 'The universal misuse of human power has the
sad effect that power, however lovingly used, is hated. To confer
benefits is surely more godlike than to ask them: yet our hearts go
out more easily to begging children than they do to generous
masters. We have so mishandled the sceptre of God which we
have usurped, we have played providence so tyrannically to one
another, that we are made incapable of loving the government of
God himself, or feeling the caress of an almighty kindness.'*

Only God's utter abandonment, then, of his almightiness will do,
if we are to come to learn to love him again. And the baby was
born in a stable, wrapped tight in swaddling clothes, and laid in a
manger, because there was no room in the inn.

 *Mary holds her finger out, and a divine hand closes on it. The master of
the world is born a begging child; he begs for milk, and does not even
know that it is milk for which he begs. We will not lift our hands to pull
the love of God down to us, but he lifts his hands to pull human
compassion down upon his cradle.*
Austin Farrer*

FRIDAY
Shepherds

Luke 2.8-12

And there were shepherds living out in the fields near by, keeping watch over their flocks at night. An angel of the Lord appeared to them, and the glory of the Lord shone around them, and they were terrified. But the angel said to them, "Do not be afraid. I bring you good news of great joy that will be for all the people. Today in the town of David a Saviour has been born to you; he is Christ the Lord. This will be a sign to you: You will find a baby wrapped in cloths and lying in a manger."

Jesu, I offer to thee here my pipe,
My skirt, my tabor, and my scrip:
Home to my felowes now will I skip,
And also look unto my shepe.
Ut hoy!
For in his pipe he made so much joy.*

So sings Joly Wat in a delightful if little sung carol, as he makes the gift of his poverty, his pipe which is his dearest treasure, and pretty well everything else he is carrying and wearing, and then flings himself home near-naked to his fellows and the sheep on the fell.

The best carols, old or new, manage to combine a rhythm and rumbustiousness that reflect their origins as dance music to celebrate the feast with sudden shafts of insight and poignancy that bring out its deeper meaning – the heat in the snowy steps of the saint, the awesome vista of 'Alpha and Omega he', the almost offhand reference to the berry as red as Christ's blood.

The gospel story too blends deep import with the warp and weft of everyday life, and the shepherds have always given nativity players the chance to let their hair down. Their work in Jesus' time made them unclean – in both senses of the word – so they had little choice but to stay out in the fields. But there is more. William Barclay stopped me in my tracks when he reminded me that many of the flocks around Bethlehem would be destined for sacrifice at the Temple.* The shepherd boy in the bleak midwinter gives a lamb to the child: the child is the lamb to be slain for the boy.

Once again we are looking at the divine exchange, the mutuality that seems built in to the work of Christ. We give him worth (worship is worth-ship), but it is through him that we are counted worthy, because to him we too are 'worth it' as the L'Oreal advert proclaims.

In our relative riches we have lost sight of our continuing poverty, and fail to either relieve it in others or see its challenge and its gift in ourselves. Only when we understand our poverty will we appreciate Christ's riches. It takes the sudden intractable disease, the desperate accident, the persistent destitute at the door to shock us out of our world of comfort and control – and into the place where we may again discover Christ to be.

 Mine are riches from your poverty,
From your innocence, eternity;
Mine forgiveness by your death for me,
Child of sorrows for my joy.
Michael Perry*

STUDY NOTES FOR WEEK FOUR
Taking Time Together

Your table will now have four candles to light, and I suggest you set up a crib set alongside them. During the week we have been thinking about gifts: perhaps each group member could bring an object that represents something they are offering in Christ's service, and explain what it means.

The crib set will have the usual characters in it. Your discussion could be based around taking each one out in turn and talking about them. What was the first Christmas like from their point of view? What did they 'bring to the party'? That could lead on to some encouragement to each other to see that each person in the group also has something that are they are contributing to God's work: we all seem to need a good deal of affirmation, and the stress levels at Christmas make that even more the case.

In fact, how can you not just as individuals but as church do a bit more to show your encouragement and appreciation of people (without making them die of embarrassment)?

Prayer time, and though you are probably sick to death of Christmas Carols by now, why not listen to a good recording of some quietly, and really try to let the words speak to you. An alternative would be to ask a group member with a good voice to read the all-too-well-known Christmas gospel passages for you in the same way. This might be a good time to remember people in prayer for whom Christmas will be a difficult time – and that might prompt a bit of action afterwards too.

CHRISTMAS DAY

The Light of the Word

Blessed are you, Sovereign Lord, King of Peace:
to you be praise and glory for ever!
The new light of your incarnate word
gives gladness in our sorrow,
and a presence in our isolation.
Fill our lives with your light,
until they overflow with gladness and praise.
Blessed be God for ever.*

'Here it is, Merry Christmas ...'* I love the upbeat lyrics and catchy tune – but **here it is**. Not just 'Merry Christmas' but the moment of moments, the time when time met eternity, when history paused for breath and the fallen world turned to begin its slow climb back to salvation.

So we must pause too, our breath taken away by the wonder of it all, and then shout: shout for our family, shout for our neighbour, shout for joy, shout: 'Christ the Lord: it is he.'*

And so there came a deep silence and the whole earth was still. The voices of the prophets and apostles were hushed, for the prophets had delivered their message, whereas the time for the apostles' preaching was yet to come. Between the two proclamations a period of silence intervened, and in the midst of this silence the Father's all-powerful Word leaped down from his royal throne ... I pray that the Word of the Lord may come again this night to those who wait in silence, and that we may know what the Lord is saying to us in our hearts.

Julian of Vezelay*

WEEK 5 MONDAY

Where is the one?

Matthew 2.1-2

After Jesus was born in Bethlehem in Judea, during the time of King Herod, Magi from the east came to Jerusalem and asked, "Where is the one who has been born king of the Jews? We saw his star in the east and have come to worship him."

Holy days and holidays: the world has a different feel in the quiet days between Christmas and New Year as we eat and drink our way through a larderful of food, play the new games, read the new books, fall out, make up – and maybe look out of the window onto a scene silent with snow.

'Real life' may seem a step or two away, but we are on our way to an Epiphany, which is all about the revelation of Christ to a very real world of politics and power; and this week has to be about helping Christmas to be a lively beginning of our mission, not a stepping stone to the sales.

Let me ease you in gently:

> *King John was not a good man,*
> *And no good friends had he.*
> *He stayed in every afternoon …*
> *But no-one came to tea.*
> *And, round about December,*
> *The cards upon his shelf*
> *Which wished him lots of Christmas cheer,*
> *And fortune in the coming year,*
> *Were never from his near and dear,*
> *But only from himself.**

It's probably awfully irreverent, but once you've put King Herod and King John in the same compartment in your mind, it's hard to get them out again. Herod in fact was a figure of considerable fun throughout the Middle Ages, played with impossible bombast (hence 'to out-Herod Herod') to guffaws all round.

The psychologists would have a field day. This is the sort of treatment we give our darkest frights to make them seem less fearsome. The massacre of the innocents was not funny. It is also a way of shifting the spotlight from ourselves, and projecting onto Herod the all-too-real horrors of our own inner natures, from our tragicomic selfishness to the times when we shut the door in the faces of others, and leave ourselves locked outside.

So we are Herod too, and John – and need to consider how we will receive the message of the magi. Are we still open to sharing in the journey, finding answers to the questions, taking another route through life? Or is our adventure over – and little surprise then if no-one seems to want to join us in it?

It will be an effort, tight as my tummy is with turkey, to get up for early prayers – but I must. It will be an effort not to fob off the down-and-out on the doorstep – but there is a journey there that I must take too. It will be an effort to lift the worship in church, now that the angels have gone away, – but when we do, what a wonder! Earth may be sleeping, but heaven is wide awake, and invites us to the party.*

There came from the East wise men, Gentiles, and that concerns us, for so are we … They came a long journey, and they came an uneasy journey. They came now, at the worst season of the year: And we, what excuse shall we have, if we come not? If so short and easy a way we come not, as from our chambers hither?

Lancelot Andrewes*

TUESDAY
In Bethlehem

Matthew 2.3-8

When King Herod heard this he was disturbed, and all Jerusalem with him. When he had called together all the people's chief priests and teachers of the law, he asked them where the Christ was to be born. "In Bethlehem in Judea," they replied, "for this is what the prophet has written:

" 'But you, Bethlehem, in the land of Judah,

are by no means least among the rulers of Judah;

for out of you will come a ruler who will be the shepherd of my people Israel.'"

Then Herod called the Magi secretly and found out from them the exact time the star had appeared. He sent them to Bethlehem and said, "Go and make a careful search for the child. As soon as you find him, report to me, so that I too may go and worship him."

If Luke saw himself as writing history, Matthew's narratives draw more on the Jewish narrative elaborations of *haggadah* and *midrash*. The *midrash* on the birth of Moses brings in a virgin birth,

magi and massacre; that on Abraham has a star and a massacre too. But this is not just a matter of Jewish folk-tales. Virgil has Aeneas follow a star to the site where Rome is to be founded; real magi visited Rome to attend the birth of Nero; and Tacitus, Suetonius and Josephus all report a belief of the time that a universal ruler was soon to arise in Judaea.*

So, cast though it is in folkloric form, today's scene is a plausible glimpse of life in a Mediterranean court of the time – and we can see why the ruling king might be disturbed.

Prophecy, as such, is at something of a discount today. But for prophecy substitute warnings of global warming – and consider how hard it is for modern administrations to know quite what to do with them. Like governments everywhere, Herod's court commissions a report ...

Nor are the problems any the less acute for today's governments where the intrusive element is not a scientific statement of fact but a religious statement of faith. What authority do holy books have now? How do we handle the competing claims of different faiths, and the tension between them all and atheism? What council is competent to be called together to decide the issues? Are we driven not only to a separation of state and religion, but a totally privatized view of religion as well; and for how long can such a state of affairs survive?

So, lurking between the lines of the story is the question as to how we as Christians should handle scripture – and in particular those parts of it which claim to direct our actions in a public as well as private way, when we live in a society which is open to all faiths and none.

This is a huge contemporary debate of international importance. All we can say, considering this passage at the moment, is that the idea of an over-arching purpose for the world, framed by Christ's coming in creation and in judgement, foretold in prophecies, birthed in Bethlehem, and definitive for our own destiny, is an irreducible factor in our faith. Just going home is not an option for us, any more than it was for the magi. But like them too we may find ourselves treading some unfamiliar ways.

Creator of the heavens,
who led the Magi by a star
to worship the Christ-child:
guide and sustain us,
that we may find our journey's end
in Jesus Christ our Lord.
Additional Collect for the Epiphany*

WEEK 5

WEDNESDAY

Bow down and worship

Matthew 2.9-12

After they had heard the king, they went on their way, and the star they had seen in the east went ahead of them until it stopped over the place where the child was. When they saw the star, they were overjoyed. On coming to the house, they saw the child with his mother Mary, and they bowed down and worshipped him. Then they opened their treasures and presented him with gifts of gold and of incense and of myrrh. And having been warned in a dream not to go back to Herod, they returned to their country by another route.

… Were we led all that way for
Birth or Death? There was a Birth, certainly,
We had evidence and no doubt. I had seen birth and death,
But had thought they were different: this Birth was
Hard and bitter agony for us, like Death, our death. *

The point of the magi's journey is not to watch, or even to wonder, but to worship. In the world of political realities that implies a choice, with consequences. Which leader shall I follow? Which creed espouse? T. S. Eliot captures the discomfort of this choice, as the very system of superstition which had brought the magi to the birth has to be abandoned by them, let die, in the face of it. Eliot is not unaware either of the close connection in Christian theology between Christ's birth and Christ's death, the need to always be holding one close to the other in liturgy as in life – so that we are always aware that Jesus is born to die, and dies for our new birth.

The wise men leave with their wisdom out-shone by the presence of Wisdom itself. They have been led by their old wisdom to the place of worship, ironically proving more faithful as the successors of Daniel's Persian opponents than his own descendants in the faith. But their triumph is only at the price of a worship that turns their wisdom upside-down.

Part of our own journey of worship – and without implying for a moment that all faith is irrational and all learning futile – is often to let Christ's light lead us to simple truths that can illuminate the complexities of our lives.

> *Step softly, under snow or rain,*
> *To find the place where men can pray:*
> *The way is all so very plain*
> *That we may lose the way.*
> *Oh, we have learnt to peer and pore*
> *On tortured puzzles from our youth,*
> *We know all labyrinthine lore.*
> *We are the three wise men of yore,*
> *And we know all things but the truth.**

Again, because it is easy to be misheard here, it is not the case that everything complex is diabolical, and that we must be simplistic to be saved. Not simplistic – but with simplicity, a simplicity of faith and worship that will give profundity to our puzzling, not pretend the puzzles are not there. Our faith, as Anselm would have put it, seeks and informs our understanding, rather than our understanding explaining and justifying our faith. We can see the difference in the eyes of the saints.

The gifts the magi first brought to Bethlehem are still being offered by all who come to Christ in faith. When we acclaim Christ as King of the universe we bring him gold from the treasury of our hearts; when we believe that the only-begotten of God has become one with human nature, we are offering myrrh for his embalming; and when we declare him to be equal in majesty to the Father, we are offering the incense of our worship before him.

Leo the Great*

THURSDAY
Orders to kill

Matthew 2.13-18

When they had gone, an angel of the Lord appeared to Joseph in a dream. "Get up," he said, "take the child and his mother and escape to Egypt. Stay there until I tell you, for Herod is going to search for the child to kill him."

So he got up, took the child and his mother during the night and left for Egypt, where he stayed until the death of Herod. And so was fulfilled what the Lord had said through the prophet: "Out of Egypt I called my son."

When Herod realised that he had been outwitted by the Magi, he was furious, and he gave orders to kill all the boys in Bethlehem and its vicinity who were two years old and under, in accordance with the time he had learned from the Magi. Then what was said through the prophet Jeremiah was fulfilled:

"A voice is heard in Ramah,
weeping and great mourning,
Rachel weeping for her children
and refusing to be comforted,
because they are no more."

All my heart this night rejoices.
As I hear, far and near,
Sweetest angel voices:
'Christ is born!' their choirs are singing,
'Till the air everywhere
Now with joy is ringing.*

The horror of the voice in Ramah can only be fully felt when we set it like this against the angel voices of the Nativity. The darkness does not snuff out the light. Paul Gerhardt wrote the words of this hymn after being expelled from his pastorate on political grounds and while mourning the death of his wife and four of their five children. But neither does the coming of the light immediately dispel all the darkness. At first, indeed, the light reveals it, contradicts it and confronts it, and conflict ensues.

Matthew is still in folk-tale mode, and it can be no accident that we find Joseph, dreams and Egypt all together in this one story.

It is hard to know how much history there is here, especially when we know that around and beyond the biblical narrative – which is quite restrained and spare – there are other episodes far more fantastic: statues falling at the child's approach, caves whose openings are covered by miraculous spiders to conceal him, and more.* History, though, does document all too many acts of slaughter by Herod, and no amount of embroidery can conceal the bloody nature of Christ's birth. No more can all the tinsel of Christmas cover up the pain of bereavement, loss and absence that so many people feel in this 'festive season'.

There is no particular virtue in having our noses rubbed into the dark side of life. Our strong temptation, though, is not this, but to discreetly avoid it. Not every church service needs to be a lament, but sometimes it feels as though we have lost the ability to lament at all. If we need to learn again how to praise with abandon, we also need to learn again how to declare the pain of abandonment. If our worship is not open to the extremes we will not so much be balanced as banal. Our private prayers should reach out to God in heaven and confront the devil in hell. Our public services should be where society around us knows that the deep realities of both its triumphs and its tragedies can be safely expressed.

Feasts like that of the Innocents are times to take a reality check on our spirituality, and seek again the fullness of life for which Christ – and his fellow-children – died.

He will come, will come
Will come like crying in the night.
Like blood, like breaking,
As the earth writhes to toss him free.
He will come like child.
Rowan Williams*

In a town called Nazareth

Matthew 2.19-23

After Herod died, an angel of the Lord appeared in a dream to Joseph in Egypt and said, "Get up, take the child and his mother and go to the land of Israel, for those who were trying to take the child's life are dead."

So he got up, took the child and his mother and went to the land of Israel.

But when he heard that Archelaus was reigning in Judea in place of his father Herod, he was afraid to go there. Having been warned in a dream, he withdrew to the district of Galilee, and he went and lived in a town called Nazareth. So was fulfilled what was said through the prophets: "He will be called a Nazarene."

One more angel, two more dreams, and a final fulfilment of prophecy, and Matthew's infancy stories come to an end, and Christmas and Epiphany are over.

Something has gone awry with this last prophecy, because there seems to be no such verse in the Old Testament. 'Nezer' is the Hebrew word for 'Branch', a title of the Messiah, and perhaps the reference is to a prophecy such a that in Isaiah 11;* but the point of the prophecy here and of the narrative as a whole is to leave us firmly in Nazareth, the place in which Jesus will grow up, and the Branch have his roots.

Where do you find yourself now – rooted, or unsettled? Like Christ you may have been displaced, transplanted – perhaps many times. There is a proper nostalgia for our deeper roots, but there is also a proper attention to the place where we are now, in the present.

Back in the first week of these reflections I mentioned that the churches in my present home city of Carlisle had given an impressive lead in responding to our recent floods, working together on the front line, touching lives, and rather surprising the civic authorities whose own infrastructure was badly hit. It is, I think, no accident that for the few years previous Christians from many Carlisle churches had been coming together to 'Pray for the City'.

(More recently the hardpressed Chief Executive of a local NHS Trust came to speak and was, I was told, amazed to see so many young people from many churches there just to listen and pray.) Real attempts are being made to heal historic rifts between churches (this is border country!) and to build bridges between the churches and the wider community, which can easily lead parallel lives. There is still a long way to go.

In my mind too is the experience of the Eden Project, not the biodomes but the blessing a great influx of young people brought to some of the more run-down areas of Manchester, both by helping with a clean-up but more importantly moving in to stay. A friend's daughter is one of them: she is working as a bouncer (!)

to keep close to the community while also using her skills to help grow a young church there. Her parents tell me that the estate where she lives is getting much better now, and it is some time since they heard gunfire in the background when they talked to her on the telephone …

No names here because she would be the first to say that this should just be the usual work of every Christian – blessing the place where we find ourselves in the present. How can that be true for you?

Why is the grass always greener for me, Lord,
on the other side of the fence,
on the future side of now?
Looking back, I thrill to your providence;
looking round, I can hardly believe all my blessings;
and still I keep looking over the fence into the future.
Give me the grace, Lord, to be where I am,
to find your blessings there,
and bless the others there too.

SATURDAY

The Word made Flesh

John 1.1-14

In the beginning was the Word, and the Word was with God, and the Word was God. He was with God in the beginning.

Through him all things were made; without him nothing was made that has been made. In him was life, and that life was the light of men. The light shines in the darkness, but the darkness has not understood it.

There came a man who was sent from God; his name was John. He came as a witness to testify concerning that light, so that through him all men might believe. He himself was not the light; he came only as a witness to the light. The true light that gives light to every man was coming into the world.

He was in the world, and though the world was made through him, the world did not recognise him. He came to that which was his own, but his own did not receive him. Yet to all who received him, to those who believed in his name, he gave the right to become children of God – children born not of natural descent, nor of human decision or a husband's will, but born of God.

The Word became flesh and made his dwelling among us. We have seen his glory, the glory of the One and Only, who came from the Father, full of grace and truth.

The way that I have structured this book means that I very nearly left out what must be the most evocative Christmas reading of all, but here it is! I've lost count of the number of times that I have taken my turn in the procession of readers, privileged as Rector to read this last and most moving of the lections, the congregation standing to receive the Word in the word, and my hairs standing on the back of my neck too.

Can I suggest you actually read it out loud, now, for yourself, slowly, giving it time to speak to you even as you speak it?

Now the Word is loose in the world. The light has been lit, the darkness is in retreat, and there is no going back. In the old high-church tradition, where my own roots lie, it used to be the custom to read this very lesson every week, as a second Gospel at the end of the Communion service, to send the people out with the Word-made-flesh that they had received in communion ringing in their ears to be lived out in their lives.

Tomorrow will be the first Sunday of a New Year, and very likely you will yourself be celebrating the presence of Christ in that Holy Communion. Could you take some time now to prepare for it, to receive again the Word made flesh, in bread and wine. It's not something we find time often enough to do.

And is it true? And is it true,
This most tremendous tale of all,
Seen in a stained-glass window's hue,
A Baby in an ox's stall?
The maker of the stars and sea
Become a child on earth for me?

And is it true? For if it is,
No loving fingers tying strings
Around those tissued fripperies,
The sweet and silly Christmas things,
Bath salts and inexpensive scent
And hideous tie so kindly meant,

No love that in a family dwells,
No carolling in frosty air,
Nor all the steeple-shaking bells
Can with this single Truth compare –
That God was Man in Palestine
And lives to-day in Bread and Wine.

John Betjeman*

WEEK 5

STUDY NOTES FOR WEEK FIVE
Taking Time Together

You'll be able to add a big extra candle to your table now for Christ himself, the Light of the World. Most of us have connections with other parts of the planet: this week each group member could bring an object along that represents such a contact (anything from a postcard to a pot), put it on the table, and tell the story of the link.

There has been some fairly meaty material in this week's reflections: Jesus didn't come into a world which was short of things that needed saving, and it still looks that way now. So what are the most important concerns that group members have about the world and its peoples today? What charities are they supporting, what campaigns? Did anyone give goats for Christmas?

Which leads, of course, to the question as to whether we as churches are awake enough to the world's needs, especially in those ones where the pressure is on just to keep the inner working of the church going and pay the bills. Better to do one thing well than ten things badly: what one thing would you like to see your church do in the coming year (try and agree!) to help bring light to the world?

That should give you plenty to pray about! But do remember once again to 'take time' to listen as well as to speak. Karl Jenkins 'The Armed Man: A Mass for Peace' is powerfully evocative of the human condition that calls out for Christ's salvation.

THE EPIPHANY
The Light of the World

O God, who by the leading of a star
manifested your only Son to the peoples of the earth:
mercifully grant that we,
who know you now by faith,
may at last behold your glory face to face;
through Jesus Christ your Son our Lord,
who is alive and reigns with you,
in the unity of the Holy Spirit,
one God, now and for ever. Amen.*

Have you ever wondered why so many early paintings of the birth show the kings not the shepherds? It was the revealing of Christ's identity at the Epiphany that counted in the early centuries of our faith, not the bare fact of his birth, which became more important as the theology of the incarnation was worked out. (The fact that many patrons of that art were kings may also have had something to do with it …)*

Liturgically, the Epiphany celebrates not only the revelation of Christ's nature to the magi, but the revelations of his identity at his baptism and in his first miracle at Cana, turning water into wine.

On January 6th, then, it would not be inappropriate to open a bottle of wine to celebrate the revelation of Christ – and to ponder how well we are doing in letting Christ turn the wateriness of our own lives into the maturity of his image. The point is not just as Christ was born sharing our human life, but that he came also to transform it into the life of heaven. Now that's a toast worth drinking to!

The Presentation

Luke 2.21-24

On the eighth day, when it was time to circumcise him, he was named Jesus, the name the angel had given him before he had been conceived.

When the time of their purification according to the Law of Moses had been completed, Joseph and Mary took him to Jerusalem to present him to the Lord (as it is written in the Law of the Lord, "Every firstborn male is to be consecrated to the Lord"), and to offer a sacrifice in keeping with what is said in the Law of the Lord: "a pair of doves or two young pigeons".

I suppose we could have stopped at the Epiphany. But there is good reason to go on – because life goes on, and neither the story of Christ nor our own story is over. Nor is the season complete in terms of the church year as it is now defined. Epiphanytide runs right on to Candlemas, February 2nd, the Feast of the Presentation of Christ in the Temple, which we read of today. Only then, at the end of the Candlemas service, are the candles blown out and – after a brief interlude of 'ordinary time' we reach Ash Wednesday, Lent and the journey to Easter.

The feast is called 'Candlemas' because in early Roman liturgies the Pope led the worshippers through the streets in candle-lit procession, and in later mediaeval times candles for the year's services were brought as gifts to church and blessed.

A bit high-church for some of my readers, I suspect! But the candles were of course just the torches of the day, later becoming symbols of worship, never substitutes for it. I would like to suggest that today you 'read' the candles as a symbol of yourself as a bearer of Christ's light, and use the Candlemas themes to reflect on how well that light shines.

First, this was a time of *purification* after childbirth. A fellow cleric in our diocese recently discovered dry rot in his bathroom. A previous conversion had boxed in the plumbing very nicely – but left damp behind the casing. Only when everything was ripped out and disinfected could the everyday world of cleaning go on again – and without determined action the rot would have spread right through the house. You can work out the moral for yourself.

Secondly, it was a time of *redemption* – making a token sacrifice in place of the ancient and barbarous practice of really sacrificing the first born. In spiritual terms this leads us straight to the sacrifice of Christ, God's first born, for us. We will not 'carry a candle' for him unless we first appreciate just how much he has done for us and can do for others.

And thirdly, it was a time of *offering* into the Lord's service. Our basic job description was given us at our baptism, and however awkward we may feel about it, it is clear that there will be an appraisal …

All this is very much the business of a well-structured 'confession' or session with a spiritual companion or director. If you don't have someone like that to talk to – perhaps it could be a New Year resolution to find one?

 Almighty and ever-living God,
clothed in majesty,
whose beloved Son was this day presented in the Temple,
in substance of our flesh:
grant that we may be presented to you
with pure and clean hearts,
by your Son Jesus Christ our Lord,
who is alive and reigns with you,
in the unity of the Holy Spirit,
one God, now and for ever.
Collect for the Feast of the Presentation*

TUESDAY
Simeon and the Spirit

Luke 2.25-28

Now there was a man in Jerusalem called Simeon, who was righteous and devout. He was waiting for the consolation of Israel, and the Holy Spirit was upon him. It had been revealed to him by the Holy Spirit that he would not die before he had seen the Lord's Christ.

Moved by the Spirit, he went into the temple courts. When the parents brought in the child Jesus to do for him what the custom of the Law required, Simeon took him in his arms and praised God, saying:

With this passage we return to one of Luke's principal themes, the work of the Holy Spirit, which we see in the lives of the righteous people who surround Christ's birth, in the life of Christ himself, and in the life of the church which follows.

We saw earlier (on page 27) how Simeon shared in the work of the 'quiet in the land' – waiting quietly for the Messiah in a time when the Spirit too was silent. Now the Spirit comes and his silence is broken.

It is hard to write about waiting on the Spirit without it seeming like a sort of remote control by God on the one hand, leaving us like those annoying but exciting radio-controlled toys that shoot round the living room at Christmas; or on the other hand just a churchy way of talking about psychology. But we have to have a go.

Taking the 'control' issue first. It seems to me that God's love for us is so strong and his purpose so fixed that, if we are at all open to them, they start to form and reform the way we think and feel and act. Most of the time this is in terms of general perceptions and preferences, but just occasionally something very specific seems to be highlighted – the need to visit someone, or suggest some word of wisdom to them, and the results make it clear that God was at work. But this is guidance and gift, not control. God has given us freedom, and is not going to take it back.

Is all this just psychology, though, by another name? In one sense, yes: anything spiritual that has a material effect must at some point be materially mediated, and so is part of the working of our bodily nature, even if it is not easily analysed by the scientific method. I am basically pro-science: but if it has a fault here it is to assume that what cannot be easily measured and analysed by the usual methods therefore does not exist, which is as fundamentalist a position as that of the science-scoffing literalist who rejects anything not explicitly described in the Bible. The issue is, do our definitions allow for complexities within and simplicities beyond the measurably material, or are they being set up in such a way that they require a reductionist point of view? I don't believe they have to be.

I hope I haven't lost you … What I want to do is leave you with the simple hope that you will do all you can to be open to the Spirit and let your life be part of the story he is writing in the world today. So simply – be a Simeon, take Christ in your arms, and let the Spirit speak.

The Holy Spirit writes his own gospel, and he writes it in the hearts of the faithful. All the actions, all the moments of the saints make up the gospel of the Holy Spirit. Their holy souls are the paper, their sufferings and their actions are the ink.

Jean-Pierre de Caussade*

WEEK 6

WEDNESDAY

Nunc Dimittis

Luke 2.29-35

"Sovereign Lord, as you have promised, you now dismiss your servant in peace. For my eyes have seen your salvation, which you have prepared in the sight of all people, a light for revelation to the Gentiles and for glory to your people Israel."
   The child's father and mother marvelled at what was said about him. Then Simeon blessed them and said to Mary, his mother: "This child is destined to cause the falling and rising of many in Israel, and to be a sign that will be spoken against, so that the thoughts of many hearts will be revealed. And a sword will pierce your own soul too."

Perhaps (I'll admit it) because my birthday falls on Candlemas, Simeon and his song have always had a very special place in my spirituality. Like the Benedictus in the morning, here is an evening song that I will never tire of, and a hope which I never want to lose.

We don't so often read the prophecy which follows, but it reminds us that this encounter was about endings as well as beginnings. The 'Nunc Dimittis' as the song is usually called (after its first words in Latin – the same goes for the Benedictus and Magnificat as well) is also read at funerals as the coffin leaves the church, and Simeon seems to have the intuition that his duty is now done, and he may now die in peace. Moreover, he looks at Mary and sees in the Spirit that Jesus will provoke in the nation, and in her, great pain as well as great joy. She in particular will have to bear the sorrow of losing him twice – once to his ministry, and once to the cross.

Our sophisticated energy supplies today distance the consumption of fuel from the generation of power. It is much simpler with a candle: in order for light to generated above, wax must be spent below. So far this week I have been urging you to shine as a light for Christ. Now we have to face the spiritual truth that we are consumed in the process. The sort of finding oneself that comes through faith in Christ inevitably involves also a losing of oneself.

The world of today not only offers us the chimera of cost-free energy, it also offers us the illusion of eternal life and health, prosperity and fulfilment as a simple continuation of the life we were born with. It is in no advertiser's interest to show us those who will *not* benefit from their product. But the rich get richer and the poor get poorer, while those in between float on a cloud of credit that obscures the truth about themselves and the hard ground not so far beneath.

The spiritual agenda here is to be honest about the adversity, and still seek to sing in it – 'Singing in the Rain' will do nicely as shorthand. And why is Gene Kelly singing his happy refrain? ''Cause the sun's in my heart and I'm ready for love!' So (ouch!) is the *Son* in your heart,  and are you open to *his* love? I'm sorry – it's the stuff of a slightly cringe-making Family Service, but sometimes simplest is best. I just wish I was better at keeping singing, or shining, myself.

Behold, then, the candle alight in Simeon's hands. You must light your own candles by enkindling them at his ... So come to him and be enlightened that you do not as much bear lamps as become them, shining within yourselves and radiating light to your neighbours.
Guerric of Igny*

WEEK 6 THURSDAY

Anna

Luke 2.36-38

There was also a prophetess, Anna, the daughter of Phanuel, of the tribe of Asher. She was very old; she had lived with her husband seven years after her marriage, and then was a widow until she was eighty-four. She never left the temple but worshipped night and day, fasting and praying. Coming up to them at that very moment, she gave thanks to God and spoke about the child to all who were looking forward to the redemption of Jerusalem.

Anna slips into our story from the shadows of the Temple, and then slips out again moments later. Why is she there?

The obvious answer is that she was there: despite Luke's skill as a story-teller, we do not have to assume that he made everything up! But why is she there? In the Temple?

It would be easy to be dismissive. Churches do seem to collect folk who need to be there all the time, and sometimes it is hard to see beyond what can come across as dependency. The same people lighting the same candle, day after day, asking for prayer for the same need service after service, perhaps trying to make up for the loss of a bereavement, perhaps just out of their depth (who isn't?) in the face of catastrophe?

But what is so wrong with dependency? Our instinct these days is to get people to move on, 'get a life'; but if a new treasure is being found to replace the one that is lost – what then?

Behind our attitude perhaps, too, is a distrust of religious routine, despite the fact that our lives are full of repetitions. Spiritual routines matter, though, and I wish I was better at them. The routines of daily prayer and reading the scriptures, of praying for others and keeping in touch with them, of giving to others and (the one I find hardest!) giving things up.

I like to think of Anna as one of those big seven-day candles that can be left burning day and night. Her routine strengthens her

resources, and there is not a hint of negativity in Luke's voice as he describes her worshipping, fasting and praying. We need more Annas.

Old acquaintance, church analyst, growth expert (and now fellow archdeacon to help it happen in practice) Bob Jackson recently surveyed successful congregations to see why they had grown. A questionnaire asked them to comment under a number of headings that previous research had shown to be likely growth factors. One vicar found it hard to fill in the questionnaire about enquirer's courses and all the rest. A disappointment for Bob? Not really. 'You see,' the vicar said, 'it's really all down to a group of people many years ago very seriously praying together. That's why we've grown.' The vicar was Sandy Millar of Holy Trinity Brompton, home of the Alpha course.*

Prayer: by some divine alchemy it both expends the wax of our spirituality and re-stocks it. Not so strange, though, if you think how muscles grow through use, or love deepens as it is expressed. Most of us need to be more determined about just doing some praying, and less worried about how it goes when we do. What will your pattern of prayer be this New Year?

There she is, Lord,
a sort of ecclesiastical bag-lady
shuffling round the pricket-stand,
lighting another candle,
muttering another prayer.
But she is praying,
while I poke fun.

Growing up

Luke 2.39-40

When Joseph and Mary had done everything required by the Law of the Lord, they returned to Galilee to their own town of Nazareth. And the child grew and became strong; he was filled with wisdom, and the grace of God was upon him.

Apart from the one isolated incident which follows, this note brings Luke's infancy cycle to an end. 'Joseph and Mary had done everything': there is more than a hint of what every parent experiences – that they must stand back and let the child do its own growing.

This can be painful even when the relationship is a good one. For a time the young person wants to be both a child and an adult, and wires get easily crossed; and the final leaving home is usually bittersweet. Sometimes, of course, the relationship is not a good one to start with, or goes wrong on the way, and then the pain can be excruciating as childhood affection gives way to rejection, 'after all we have done for you.'

Luke's parable of the Prodigal Son inevitably comes to mind here, and invites us to see God as the parent and ourself as the growing child. He has given us everything we have, done everything for us, and now we …

We have to re-discover God and love him as adults, and a prodigal's journey is part of our normal spiritual growth. But how can growing apart and growing up in God fit together, and how can it be more than just our own enterprise?

Luke speaks of strength, wisdom and grace as marks of growth, and all of these are words associated with the Holy Spirit, with God's action in us. Growing, *apart* from God without growing away from him, can happen because *a part* of God has become part of us, so that our growing is neither our work nor his but ours together. Paul wrestles with this in Romans chapters 6 to 8, and ends up saying that, 'The Spirit himself testifies with our spirit that we are God's children.'*

I am avoiding the language of 'filling', not because I don't believe in it but because the Spirit does not just power us like petrol but is with us as a person, joined to our deepest personal being. Perhaps a better image is the memory of a loved one that we carry within us so powerfully that we are shaped by it. Paul has a similar picture when he speaks in 2 Corinthians of God setting his seal of ownership on us as he puts his Spirit in our hearts,* where the point is that the seal imprints itself on us.

A seal's imprint is usually on wax – and we are back to candles. Even a seven-day candle burns low and however strong our spiritual discipline it will not route-march us back to God. Nor are we just to be topped up with new wax and carry on as before. No – we are re-melted, re-made and renewed as we become more and more like Christ, until it become impossible to speak of our light or his apart.

In my family, whenever things get tough we phone home, and in long conversations we are rebuilt and draw on one another to find new strength, wisdom and grace. Do remember to phone home – we usually call it prayer.

Almighty Father,
whose Son our Saviour Jesus Christ is the light of the world:
may your people,
illumined by your word and sacraments,
shine with the radiance of his glory,
that he may be known, worshipped, and obeyed to the ends of the earth;
for he is alive and reigns, now and for ever.
Post-communion Collect for the Third Sunday of Epiphany*

WEEK 6

SATURDAY

At the Temple

Luke 2.41-52
Every year his parents went to Jerusalem for the Feast of the Passover. When he was twelve years old, they went up to the Feast, according to the custom. After the Feast was over, while his parents were returning home, the boy Jesus stayed behind in Jerusalem, but they were unaware of it. Thinking he was in their company, they travelled on for a day. Then they began looking for him among their relatives and friends. When they did not find him, they went back to Jerusalem to look for him. After three days they found him in the temple courts, sitting among the teachers, listening to them and asking them

questions. Everyone who heard him was amazed at his understanding and his answers. When his parents saw him, they were astonished. His mother said to him, "Son, why have you treated us like this? Your father and I have been anxiously searching for you."

"Why were you searching for me?" he asked. "Didn't you know I had to be in my Father's house?" But they did not understand what he was saying to them.

Then he went down to Nazareth with them and was obedient to them. But his mother treasured all these things in her heart. And Jesus grew in wisdom and stature, and in favour with God and men.

Many miraculous stories were soon in circulation about the boyhood of Christ, and since most of them ring about as true as an old school bell, it is a mercy that the Council of Nicaea kept them out of the canon.

The scriptures give us just this one. It has the authentic feel of real family life and a note of deep portent. It is the Passover – Jesus will be in Jerusalem again for this one day. But this is now his *bar mitzvah*, when he becomes a Son of the Law in his own right, and he is found listening and learning about it.

Mary's tone of voice, however, is far from reverent! Jesus may be growing up, but he is still young and the time for the separation we talked of yesterday has not yet properly come.

The story acts a bridge between infancy and ministry, a foretaste of pains still to come. It stands helpfully at the end of this short book, as 'ordinary time' begins again.

New Year's Day should be between a week and a fortnight in the past now, and most of us will be back in our ordinary routines. What about those resolutions? A lot of them, let's be honest, are a waste of time, but ones will not be wasted which plant within us something of the special-ness of the season we are leaving, so that we do not face a Narnian 'winter but never Christmas' but an echo of Christmas even in high summer. And the seeds that will bear fruit are not sentimental reminiscences but sound spiritual disciplines which keep our story with God moving on.

Let's look back. What are the pointers of promise that God has given you, and are you recollecting them? If alarm bells are ringing in your life, are you finding yourself able to look for God's call in them? Are you preparing God's way like the Baptist? Are you keeping the Christ-child in your gaze, taking his light out into the world, and keeping your light shining?

Answer yes to too many of these questions and I will refuse to believe you! But I hope you will carry on trying to answer them, and that I will too. We still have a big part to play in this story, candles in the dark maybe, but shining with a light that can save the world.

God our creator,
who in the beginning
commanded the light to shine out of darkness:
we pray that the light of the glorious gospel of Christ
may dispel the darkness of ignorance and unbelief,
shine into the hearts of all your people,
and reveal the knowledge of your glory in the face of Jesus Christ
your Son our Lord,
who is alive and reigns with you,
in the unity of the Holy Spirit,
one God, now and for ever.
Collect for the Fourth Sunday of Epiphany*

STUDY NOTES FOR WEEK SIX

Taking Time Together

So what goes on the table, now that the decorations have come down? Our theme has been 'Light for our Lives', so how about just keeping the Christ candle, but setting it on a map of your area. Use tiddlywinks or the like to mark the places where you live and work, shop and go to school, have fun and meet friends, explaining as you go.

What is it like living in your spot these days? We looked at the big issues of the world last week, but there will be pressing ones close to home as well. What are they? In Carlisle, for instance, there's a big debate about how to rebuild after the floods. What will make it a great city for the future? What does your village, town or city need to be a bit further on the way towards the kingdom of God? What things are group members engaged in to help it do that?

And … what can you and should you be doing together, as church ?

This is the end of your 'Time Together', so it would be good to pray for one another, and perhaps set up some simple way of keeping on sharing your prayer concerns. You might consider each writing down yours on a postcard now, putting that on the table, and then praying not for your own needs but ones others have shared. Then how about a Bach organ fugue or two to listen to as you continue to let your prayers interweave with each silently while you listen to the music? Mark the ending with some prayers to say together and a song if you sing – and Lent isn't far away if taking time together has helped.

References

viii For the history of the Advent wreath and its use in current liturgy see Michael Perham and Kenneth Stevenson, *Welcoming the Light of Christ* (SPCK, London 1991) esp. pp.44 & 52. The book is a companion to the Church of England's service book for the season from All Saints to Candlemas, *The Promise of His Glory* (Church House Publishing/Mowbray, London 1991)

ix R.S. Thomas, 'Kneeling' in *Selected Poems 1946-1968* (Hart-Davis MacGibbon, London, 1973) p.119

x *Common Worship: Services and Prayers for the Church of England* (Church House Publishing, London 2000) p.376

1 Candle prayer from *Promise of His Glory* p.137

7 Gerard Manley Hopkins, 'God's Grandeur' in *Poems* ed. W.H. Gardner & N. H. Mackenzie (OUP London, 4th ed. 1970) p.66

7 Peter Chysologus, Sermon 160, in Robert Atwell, *Celebrating the Seasons* (Canterbury Press, Norwich 1999) p.67. This passage and some others I use are cited by Michael Perham, *Glory in our Midst* (SPCK, London 2005). I am greatly indebted to both books in helping me to gather material for the prayer sections of these reflections.

8 Wilfred Owen, 'The Parable of the Old Man and the Young', in *Collected Poems ed*. C. Day Lewis (Chatto & Windus, London 1964) p.42

10 T S Eliot , 'Four Quartets – Little Gidding', in *Complete Poems and Plays* (Faber & Faber, London & Boston 1969) p.192

13 John V Taylor, *The Christ-like God* (SCM, London 1992)

13 *Common Worship* p.376

15 Candle prayer from Promise of His Glory p.137

19 The pundit was David Aaronovitch.

19 Ann Lewin, 'Incarnation' in *Watching for the Kingfisher* (Methodist Publishing House , London 2004)

21 George Herbert, 'Elixer' in *The English Poems of George Herbert* ed. C. A. Patrides (Dent, London 1974) p.188, sung as the hymn 'Teach me, my God and King'

21 P. D. James, *Death in Holy Orders* (Faber & Faber, London 2001) p.200

21 Rick Warren, *The Purpose Driven Life* (Zondervan, Grand Rapids 2002) p.318

21 G. A. Studdart-Kennedy, 'Patience' cit. Cyril Bulley, *Glimpses of the Divine* (Churchman, Worthing 1987) under Nov. 24th

23 The acronym FTCW is used by the London Institute for Contemporary Christianity www.licc.org.uk

23 Henry Vaughan 'The Dawning', *Poems* ed. E.K. Chambers (Routledge, London n.d.) i. p.124

24 eg Gen 1.2; Dt 34.9; Luke 3.22; Luke 4.1; Rom 5.5; Eph 5.18

25 George Matheson, 'O Love that wilt not let me go', *Common Praise* (Canterbury Press, Norwich 2000) no. 542

26 Quoted by William Barclay, *Gospel of Matthew* (St Andrew Press, Edinburgh 1956) p.35. It was part of Jewish self-understanding that after the canonical prophets formal prophecy ceased and only the daughter or echo of the voice was heard.

26 Luke 2.25-6. On 'The Quiet in the Land' see William Barclay again, *The Gospel of Luke* (St Andrew Press, Edinburgh, 1953) p.21

27 Sue McClellan, John Pac, Keith Ryecroft, 'Colours of Day' in *Come and Praise* (BBC, London 1978) p.80

29 Candle prayer from *Promise of His Glory* p.138

29 C.S. Lewis, *The Lion, the Witch and the Wardrobe* (rep. Puffin, Harmondsworth 1959) p.98

31 *Common Worship* p.378

35 Ambrose of Milan, Commentary on St John's Gospel, in Robert Atwell, *Celebrating the Seasons* (Canterbury Press, Norwich 1999) p.38

36 Boris Pasternak, *Dr Zhivago* trans. Max Hayward and Manya Harari (Collins, London, 1958)

37 Augustine of Hippo, Sermon 293, *Celebrating the Seasons* p.23

41 *Common Worship* p.378

43 Candle Prayer from *Promise of His Glory* p.139

43 The Church Army promotes posada in the UK, and figures are available from the charity Toybox.

45 Robert Southwell, The Nativity of Christ, *Celebrating the Seasons* p.49

45 Paraphrasing of course George Bernard Shaw

45 See reflections on this painting in John Drury, *Painting the Word* (Yale UP, New Haven 1999) p.48 and my *Lent with Luke* (Authentic, Carlisle 2005) p.4

45 Bernard of Clairvaux, Sermon 4 'In Praise of the Blessed Virgin Mary', *Celebrating the Seasons* p.37

47 The words of this blessing are either derived from or echoed in a prayer cited in 'The Amadan' by Fiona MacLeod (in volume 3 of the uniform edition of 1910), who was really one William Sharp of Paisley, who also published *The Pagan Review* in 1892. My intention is not at all pagan!

49 Piero della Francesca's Nativity dates from 1470-75. Giotto's fresco of 1304-6 is in the Arena Chapel, Padua; Conrad van Soest's triptych of 1403 is in the Parish Church at Bad Wildungen. Reproductions can be seen at www.biblical-art.com

51 W. H. Vanstone, *Love's Endeavour, Love's Expense* (DLT, London 1977) p.119

51 Both quotations are from Austin Farrer, Said or Sung (London 1960, pp.34-4) cit. *Celebrating the Seasons* p.40

52 'Joly Wat' in Martin Manser, *Best-loved Christmas Carols* (Collins, London 2005) p.108

53 William Barclay, *The Gospel of Luke* (St Andrew Press, Edinburgh 1953) p.17

53 Michael Perry, 'The Calypso Carol', *Common Praise* 68

54 W.H. Auden, *For the Time Being* (Faber, London 1945)

55 Basil the Great, Homily 2 'On the Nativity', *Celebrating the Seasons* p.54

57 Candle Prayer from *Promise of His Glory* p.140.

57 Noddy Holder's 'Here it is, Merry Christmas ...' was the chorus of Slade's Christmas hit in 1973. It is an acquired taste.

57 I am thinking of Pat Uhl's powerful Advent song, 'O what a gift',*Complete Mission Praise* (Marshall Pickering, London 1999) no. 526

57 Julian of Vezelay, Sermon 'On the Nativity', *Celebrating the Seasons* p.46. Julian was a twelfth century Benedictine monk.

58 A.A. Milne, 'King John's Christmas' in *Now We are Six* (Methuen, London 1927) p.2

59 'Heaven invites you to a party' is one of Graham Kendrick's songs in *Make Way for Christmas: The Gift* (Kingsway, Eastbourne 1988)

59 Lancelot Andrewes' Sermon preached before King James I at Whitehall in 1620, *Celebrating the Seasons* p.69.

60 See e.g. David Hill, *The Gospel of Matthew* (Oliphants, London 1972) pp. 80-81

61 *Additional Collects* (CHP, London 2004) p.8

62 T.S. Eliot, 'The Journey of the Magi', *Complete Poems and Plays* p.104

63 G.K. Chesterton, 'The Wise Men', *Best-loved Christmas Carols* (Collins, London 2005) p.211

63 Leo the Great, Sermon 3, 'On the Epiphany', *Celebrating the Seasons* p.72

64 Paul Gerhardt trans. Catherine Winkworth, 'All my heart', *Common Praise* no. 43

65 A selection of Infancy Gospels can be found amongst the apocryphal material in the Ante-Nicene Fathers collection on-line at www.ccel.org/fathers2/ANF-08. The story of the idolatrous statues falling in the temple of Hermopolis, for instance, is from the *Gospel of Pseudo-Matthew* ch.22.

65 Rowan Williams, 'Advent Calendar' in *After Silent Centuries* (OUP, Oxford 1996)

66 See e.g. David Hill, *The Gospel of Matthew* (Oliphants, London 1972) pp.87-88

69 John Betjeman, 'Christmas', *Best-loved Christmas Carols* (Collins, London 2005) p.40

71 Collect for The Epiphany, *Common Worship* p.383

71 See Neil's MacGregor's excellent *Seeing Salvation* (BBC, London 2000) ch. 2 for background here

73 *Common Worship* p.386

75 Jean-Pierre de Caussade, *Self-Abandonment to the Divine Providence*, cit. *Celebrating the Seasons* p.105

77 Guerric of Igny, Sermon on the Presentation of Christ in the Temple, *Celebrating the Seasons* p.112

79 Bob Jackson, *The Road to Growth* (Church House Publishing, London 2005) p.220

81 Romans 8.16; 2 Corinthians 1.22

81 *Common Worship* p.385

83 *Common Worship* p.385